Admire art, inside art.

アートの中でアートを観る。

1: ガラス技法の世界
The world of glass technique

ガラス工芸の制作工程は、溶けたガラスの形を整える「成形」、常温までゆっくり冷やして固める「徐冷」、装飾を加える「加飾」に大きく分類できます。ここでは、5種類の「加飾」の技法に着目し、その特徴を抽出したオリジナルのガラスオブジェを通して制作過程に迫ります。

※展示しているオブジェは実際に手で触れてお楽しみいただけますが、尚且お足を運びますのでお気をつけてください。
※ガラス破砕片です。オブジェを動かしたり持ち上げたりしないように配慮を願いいたします。

基本的な成形方法

約1,200度の熔解炉で、原料となる珪砂、ソーダ灰、石灰などを熔かしてガラス種をつくります。これを吹き竿の先に巻き取り、竿を回転させながら息を吹き込んでガラスを膨らませていくのが基本的な成形方法です。宙空で吹いて成形する「宙吹き」と、型の中へ吹き込んで成形する「型吹き」があります。

主な使用道具

ジャック　　ピンサー　　口切りばさみ　　横切りばさみ

ガラスを竿から外すためのひねりを入れるときなどに使う。形のわずかな調整。

ガラスの表面をつまんだり角を入れたり、パーツをつなぐときなどに使う。

竿にガラス種をつけて形を整えるのに使うはさみ。

ガラスを竿から切り離すのに使うはさみ。

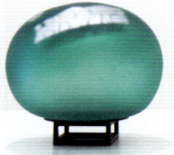

010 — 011

目の前では穏やかな瀬戸内海が、振り向けばなだらかな山々が迎え入れます。
広島県の南西部に位置する大竹市。海岸線に沿って350mほど続く約4.6haの敷地に
2023年、美術館・ヴィラ・レストランからなる複合施設「SIMOSE」が誕生しました。
建築はすべて、世界で活躍する建築家、坂 茂が設計。
この地の風景を咀嚼し、素材や構造から考え抜かれた稀有な建築群が並びます。
自分の内に風をとおすような、気持ちのいい日を過ごすための場所です。

The calm Seto Inland Sea unfolds before your eyes,
and the rolling mountains embrace you as you look back.
Otake City is located in the southwestern part of Hiroshima Prefecture.
In 2023, SIMOSE, a new complex facility consisting of
an art museum, villas, and a restaurant, was opened on a site of
approximately 4.6 hectares that stretches 350 meters along the coastline.
The site features a series of unique buildings designed by
the world-renowned architect Shigeru Ban, which examine
the regional landscape and carefully consider both materials and structures.
It is a place where you can spend a pleasant day, feeling the breeze pass through you.

下瀬美術館 ——————————————————— 018
Simose Art Museum

溶け込む建築、動く建築………020
Architecture That Blends In, Architecture That Moves

下瀬コレクション………026
The Simose Collection

望洋テラス……038
Seaview Terrace

エミール・ガレの庭………040
Emile Gallé's Garden

ミュージアムショップ………042
Museum Shop

Dialogue I アート施設とクリエイション　坂 茂 × 原 研哉………052
Art Facilities and Creation　Shigeru BAN × Kenya HARA

サインシステム………064
Signage System

Simose Art Garden Villa ————————————————— 070

レセプション棟………072
Reception

Villa 1　ダブル・ルーフの家………076
House of Double-Roof

Villa 2　壁のない家………080
Wall-Less House

Villa 3　十字壁の家………084
Cross Wall House

Villa 4　家具の家………088
Furniture House

Villa 5　紙の家………092
Paper House

Villa 6-10　キールステックの家 A-E………100
Kielsteg House A-E

SIMOSE French Restaurant ————————————————— 110

Dialogue II ヴィラ建築と瀬戸内海　坂 茂 × 原 研哉………120
Villa Architecture and Seto Inland Sea　Shigeru BAN × Kenya HARA

データ………128
Data

クレジット………134
Credit

アートに触れる場、SIMOSE　下瀬ゆみ子………136
SIMOSE: A Place to Experience Art　Yumiko SHIMOSE

全体マップ………140
Map

Contents　　　　　　　　　　　　　　016 —— 017

下瀬美術館

水盤に並ぶ多彩な可動展示室や、外壁に瀬戸内の自然を映す建築群、所蔵するエミール・ガレの作品にちなんだ庭園など、アートのような空間に身をおきながらアート作品を満喫することができる下瀬美術館。広島市に本社を構える建築資材の総合メーカー・丸井産業株式会社の代表取締役である下瀬ゆみ子が、親子2代にわたり受け継ぎながら収集してきたコレクション約500点を保存・公開しています。

Simose Art Museum

The Simose Art Museum allows visitors to fully enjoy artworks while immersing themselves in art-like spaces including colorful movable galleries perched on a water basin, a group of buildings reflecting the surrounding landscape of the Setouchi region on their outer walls, and a garden inspired by the works of Emile Gallé. Yumiko Shimose, President of Marui Sangyo —a comprehensive manufacturer of building materials based in Hiroshima City— has so far preserved and exhibited some 500 items from the collection passed down through her family for two generations.

溶け込む建築、動く建築

土地の特性や地域の文脈と向き合いながら、最小限の素材で最大限の空間を実現してきた建築家、坂 茂。下瀬美術館においても、瀬戸内海沿いに広がる開放的な敷地をいかに生かしきるかということを命題に、多様な素材と独自の構造を取り入れました。外観を特徴付けるのは、海岸線と並行に建てられた長さ180m、高さ8.5mの「ミラーガラス・スクリーン」。エントランス棟、企画展示棟、管理棟の3つの建物を一体化する自立壁です。隣接する住宅地の風景から美術館一帯の空間を切り離すと同時に、外壁の鏡面に周囲のランドスケープを映り込ませることで海や空、山や緑といった自然を増幅し、巨大な建築物を風景の中にゆるやかに溶け込ませています。

　鑑賞体験はエントランス棟からはじまります。チケットカウンターをはじめミュージアムカフェやショップのあるこの建物は、展示棟への明快な動線やテラス空間を設けるために、円形より方向性がある形態として楕円で計画されました。設計にあたり、隣接させた2つの正円を曲線でつないで楕円を描く作図

Architecture That Blends In, Architecture That Moves

Shigeru Ban is an architect who has managed to maximize spaces with minimum use of materials while dealing with specific characteristics of the land and the local context. For the Simose Art Museum, he adopted various materials and unique structures under the proposition of how to make the most of the open site along the Seto Inland Sea. The exterior is characterized by a 180-meter long, 8.5-meter high mirrored glass screen built parallel to the coastline. This freestanding wall integrates the three buildings: the entrance hall, the exhibition hall, and the administration building. It also separates the museum space from the adjacent residential landscape and amplifies the scenery of the sea, sky, mountains, and greenery by reflecting such surroundings on the mirrored glass wall, gently blending the massive buildings into the landscape.

　　　The viewing experience begins at the entrance hall. This building accommodating the ticket counter, museum cafe, and store was designed in an oval shape to make a terrace space as well as to provide a clear path to the exhibition hall considering an elliptical shape gives a clearer sense of direction than a round shape. The design adopted a drafting method in which two adjacent perfect circles are connected with curved lines to form an ellipse, and as a result, the building required a column at the center of each circle. In seeking a way to support the entire structure with a minimum number of beams

法が採用されたため、それぞれの円の中心に柱が必要となり、2点の柱から最小限の梁で全体を支える方法を求めた結果、枝を広げた大木のような傘形の構造が生まれました。形態と構造の整合性を突き詰めることで自ずと見つけ出された建築です。

　展示棟へは渡り廊下で結ばれています。ミラーガラスでできた壁は内側からはガラス張りに見えており、屋内に身をおきながら周囲の自然とつながり合う開放感がもたらされています。その景色の間にぽっかりと空いた開口部から企画展示棟へ。ポストテンション方式により実現した25×30mの大スパン空間は、可動壁でフレキシブルに区切る仕組みとなっており、雛人形やエミール・ガレ、日本と西洋の近代絵画など展示に合わせて多様な空間に変化します。企画展示棟の屋外部分にはピラミッド状の盛土が施されていますが、これもまた建築物としての存在感を軽減しランドスケープに溶け込ませるための工夫です。なだらかな坂道を登ると、丘の上にある望洋テラスへと辿り着きます。

　ふたたび屋内に入り、渡り廊下を挟んで海側に位置する可動展示室へ。水盤の上にたたずむ8つの展示室は、エミール・ガレの作品に登場する花の色から抽出された8色のカラーガラスに覆われた、それぞれ10m四方のホワイトキューブになっています。瀬戸内の多島美から着想され、広島の造船技術を活用して水の浮力で動かせる仕組みとした、世界でも類を見ない建築作品です。

from the two columns, an umbrella-shaped structure that looks like a large tree spreading its branches was born. The form was naturally found by pursuing the consistency of form and structure.

The building leads to the exhibition hall via a connecting corridor. The mirrored glass wall looks like glass from the inside, so one can feel a sense of openness and connection with the surrounding nature while being inside. Visitors enter the exhibition hall through an opening in the reflected scenery. The 25 x 30 meter large-span space, achieved by the post-tensioning system, can be flexibly divided using movable walls and can be transformed into various spaces to accommodate a variety of exhibits such as Hina Dolls, the Emile Gallé collection, and modern Japanese and Western paintings. The pyramid-shaped embankment outside the exhibition building is another ingenious idea to mitigate the building's presence and blend it into the landscape. A gentle slope leads to the Seaview Terrace on top of the hill.

Visitors return indoors once again and walk through the connecting corridor to the movable galleries on the seaward side of the building. The eight exhibition rooms, each a 10-meter square white cube, are covered with colored glass in eight different shades derived from the colors of the flowers in Emile Gallé's works. This one-of-a-kind architectural work was inspired by the beauty of the Seto Inland Sea archipelago. The structure is designed to move using a mechanism powered by water buoyancy leveraging Hiroshima's shipbuilding technology.

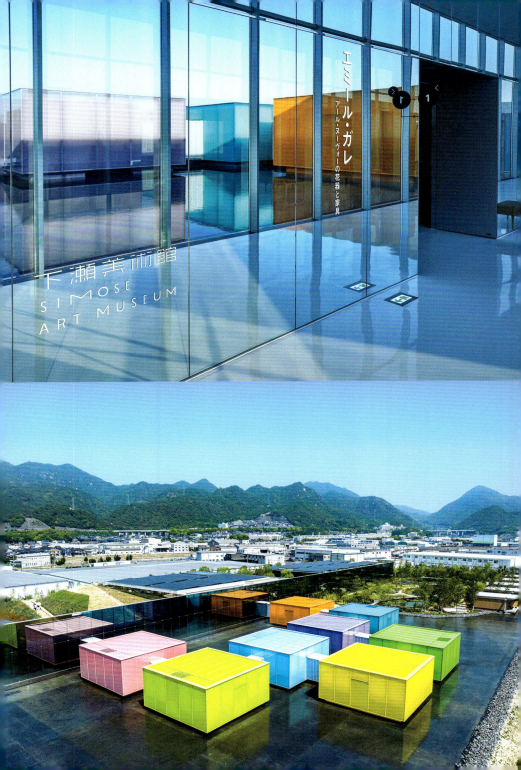

可動展示室の仕組み
How the Movable Galleries Work

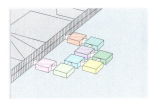 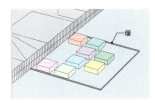 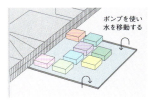

1. 展示品の移動、インフラの停止
室内を空にして、展示室への電源供給と加湿給水用配管を停める。
1. Remove exhibits and shut down infrastructure
Empty the rooms and shut off the power supply to the movable galleries and the piping for the humidifier water supply.

2. ブリッジの解体、堰の設置
ユニット化されたブリッジを一旦解体。可動範囲の縁に堰をおき、水をせき止める。
2. Dismantle bridges and place weirs
Dismantle modular bridges temporarily. Place weirs around the edges of the moving range to hold back the water.

3. 水の移動、展示室の浮き確認
水盤内蔵のポンプで、堰の内側へ水を移動。水深60cmとなり、展示室が浮上する。
3. Move the water and check how the movable galleries float up
Transfer the water to the inside of the weir using a built-in pump. The movable galleries float up when the water depth reaches 60 centimeters.

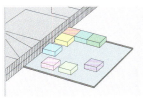 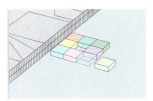 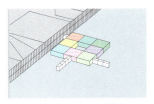

4. 展示室の移動
チェーンブロックで動きを制御し、展示室を人力で引っ張る。
4. Move the movable galleries
Use chain blocks to regulate the movements, and tow the movable galleries manually.

5. 展示室の固定、堰の撤去
固定ピンをセットし、展示室を水盤底に設置。堰を除き、水深を元に戻す。
5. Secure the movable galleries and remove the weirs
Set the anchoring pins and position the movable galleries on the bottom of the water basin. Remove the weirs and restore the water depth to the original level.

6. ブリッジの復旧、インフラの接続
ユニット化されたブリッジを再構築、加湿給水用配管を再接続する。
6. Restore bridges and reconnect infrastructure
Restore modular bridges and reconnect water supply piping for humidifiers.

移動方法と配置パターン
Moving Method and Layout Patterns

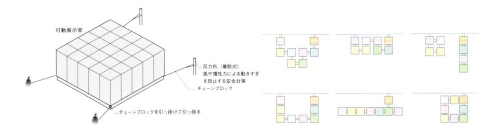

Simose Art Museum

下瀬コレクション

500点余を誇るコレクションの原点となったのは、雛人形と京人形。その多くが創業250年余の京都・丸平大木人形店の当主、大木平藏によって製作されたものであり、子どもの成長と平和な世の中を祈って集められてきました。その後、フランスのアール・ヌーヴォーを代表する工芸家、エミール・ガレを中心とした西洋工芸、日本近代や西洋の絵画へと広げられてきています。

The Simose Collection

The collection, which boasts more than 500 items, originally started with Hina Dolls and Kyoto Dolls. Many of them were made by the Maruhei Oki Doll Shop, of which Heizo Oki is the head in Kyoto, a company founded over 250 years ago, and were collected to wish for children's growth and a peaceful world. The collection has since expanded to include Western arts and crafts, particularly works of Emile Gallé, a leading French Art Nouveau craftsman, as well as modern Japanese and Western painting.

Simose Art Museum

《黒御袍立像御雛》
制作年：1975年頃
材質技法：木、布
六世大木平藏製

Hina dolls
ca. 1975
Heizo Oki VI

京人形・雛人形を中心とする工芸作品
コレクションの多数を占める分野で、約130点の京人形・雛人形と雛道具を所蔵。他にも、日本における球体関節人形のパイオニアとして知られる四谷シモンの作品、北大路魯山人や三輪休雪の陶器などを揃えています。

Craftworks Centered on Kyoto Dolls and Hina Dolls
This category, comprising the majority of the collection, features some 130 items of Kyoto Dolls, Hina Dolls, doll furnishings. Other items in the collection include works by Simon Yotsuya, known as the pioneer of ball-jointed doll in Japan, as well as ceramics by Rosanjin Kitaoji and Kyusetsu Miwa.

《染付猛鳥画花瓶》
制作年：1929年
材質技法：陶
北大路魯山人

Vase with hawk design, underglaze blue
1929
Rosanjin Kitaoji

《少女の人形》
制作年：1993年
材質技法：紙、木、ガラス、毛、布、革
四谷シモン

Girl
1993
Simon Yotsuya

東山魁夷、加山又造、小磯良平を中心とする日本近代絵画

静謐な風景画から「青の画家」と呼ばれる東山魁夷、戦後の日本画壇を導いた加山又造などの日本画を所蔵。清楚で知的な人物画を特徴とする小磯良平や、浅井忠、梅原龍三郎、佐伯祐三といった近代を代表する画家たちの油彩画もあります。

Japanese Modern Art Centered on Kaii Higashiyama, Matazo Kayama, and Ryohei Koiso

The collection features Japanese paintings by Kaii Higashiyama, known as the "blue painter" for his tranquil landscapes; Matazo Kayama, a leader of the postwar Japanese painting scene. It also includes oil paintings by prominent modern painters such as Ryohei Koiso, known for his neat and intellectual portraits, Chu Asai, Ryuzaburo Umehara, and Yuzo Saeki.

《クラマールの午後》
制作年：1925年頃
材質技法：油彩、カンヴァス、パネル
佐伯祐三

Clamart in the afternoon
ca. 1925
Yuzo Saeki

《音》
制作年：1982年
材質技法：紙本着色
加山又造

Sound
1982
Matazo Kayama

Simose Art Museum

Simose Art Museum

エミール・ガレを中心とする西洋工芸

日々の暮らしの癒しとして収集されてきたガレの作品は、ガラス器、陶器、木工家具まで60点以上を数えます。他にも、ドームのガラス器、マジョレルの家具、マイセンの磁器などを所蔵しています。

Western Crafts Centered on Emile Gallé

Gallé's works, which have been collected for giving a sense of inner peace in the collector's everyday life, includes more than 60 pieces of glassware, ceramics, and wood furniture. Other items in the collection include glassware by Daum Frères, furniture by Majorelle, and Meissen porcelain.

《蘭文脚付杯》
制作年：1900年頃
材質技法：ガラス（被せガラス、金属酸化物の封入、エッチング、グラヴュール）
エミール・ガレ

Footed cup (orchid design)
ca.1900
Emile Gallé

《ハートの涙（ケマンソウ）》
制作年：1902年頃
材質技法：ガラス（被せガラス、グラヴュール、マルケトリ、アプリカシオン）
エミール・ガレ

Dicentra Spectabilis
ca.1902
Emile Gallé

マティス、ピサロを中心とする西洋美術

19世紀後半から20世紀にかけての油彩画・版画をコレクション。ミレー、ピサロ、ルノワール、ルソー、マティスなど、主にフランスの巨匠たちによる作品が並びます。

Western Art with a Focus on Matisse and Pissarro

The collection includes oil paintings and prints from the late 19th to 20th centuries. It mainly features works by French masters such as Millet, Pissarro, Renoir, Rousseau, and Matisse.

《青いチュチュの踊り子》
制作年：1942年
材質技法：油彩、カンヴァス
アンリ・マティス

Dancer with a blue tutu
1942
Henri Matisse

《バザンクール草原・秋》
制作年：1894年
材質技法：油彩、カンヴァス
カミーユ・ピサロ

Meadows at Bazincourt, Autumn
1894
Camille Pissarro

Simose Art Museum

8: 人物の魅力
Portrait

企画展示棟と管理棟の間に現れる、通称「鏡の森」。ミラーガラスとステンレス鏡面に緑が映り込み、まるで森の中に迷い込んだかのような感覚になるかもしれません。

The so-called Mirror Forest appears between the exhibition hall and the administration building. The mirrored glass and mirror-polished stainless steel reflect the greenery, making visitors feel as if they have wandered into a forest.

望洋テラス

企画展示棟の周囲はピラミッド状に盛土され、なだらかな丘になっています。その道を登ると、一面の海景。世界遺産の厳島神社で知られる宮島をはじめ、釣りの名所として親しまれる阿多田島、旧海軍の史跡が残る江田島などの島々が眺められます。また8色の可動展示室が眼下に一望できるほか、日没後には大竹コンビナートの工場夜景も楽しめます。

Seaview Terrace

The exhibition hall is surrounded by a pyramid-shaped embankment that forms a gently sloping hill. Walking up the hill, one is greeted by sweeping views of the ocean and islands including Miyajima Island, known for the World Heritage Site of Itsukushima Shrine, Atatajima Island, a famous fishing spot, and Etajima Island, which still retains the historic sites of the former navy. It also offers a panoramic view of the movable galleries in eight different shades. The night view of the Otake Petrochemical Complex can also be enjoyed after sunset.

エミール・ガレの庭

アール・ヌーヴォーを代表する工芸家エミール・ガレは、自然をモチーフとした作品を手掛けるだけでなく、植物学者としても活動しました。そんなガレの作品に登場する草花を中心に、瀬戸内の気候に合わせて植栽された庭園です。

Emile Gallé's Garden

Emile Gallé, a decorative artist who represented Art Nouveau, not only designed works with motifs of nature, but also worked as a botanist. This garden was planted in harmony with the climate of Setouchi, centering on flowers which appear in Gallé's works of art.

Simose Art Museum

ミュージアムショップ

エントランス棟の一角にたたずむショップでは、可動展示室をモチーフにしたグラフィカルな小物をはじめ、美術館の所蔵品や施設内の建築に着想したオブジェなど、SIMOSEの記憶を日常に持ち帰ることができるオリジナルグッズを取り揃えています。

Museum Shop

The museum shop, located in a corner of the entrance hall, offers a variety of original goods so visitors can take home memories of SIMOSE, including graphical accessories inspired by the movable galleries and objects inspired by the museum's collection and the architecture within the complex.

ショップの反対側には、ミュージアムカフェも併設。鑑賞や散策のあいまに、季節のフルーツを使ったデザートや軽食、コーヒー・紅茶などが楽しめます。

Across from the shop, there is a cafe. While strolling around the museum, visitors can enjoy sweets and light meals made with seasonal fruits as well as coffee, tea, and other beverages.

SIMOSEオリジナルグッズ ガレのかけら

下瀬美術館のコレクションを代表するエミール・ガレ。そのガラス作品に見られる多様な加飾表現を、現代のガラス技法で再現したペーパーウェイトです。「カボション」「模玉ガラス」など全6種を製作しています。

SIMOSE Original Goods: Piece of Gallé
Emile Gallé represents the collection of the Simose Art Museum. These paperweights are reinterpretations of the various decorative expressions found in Gallé's glass works using contemporary glass techniques. Six types are available, including "cabochon" and "jade glass."

カボション
ガラスの表面に半球状の色ガラスを熔着し、宝石のようなアクセントを加える技法を再現。

Cabochon
A technique to add jewel-like accents to the glass surface by fusing small hemispherical colored glass pieces onto the surface.

ベースの製作　Making the Base　　　　　　　　　　　　　　　　　　　　　　　　　パーツの熔着　Fusing of Parts

吹き竿にガラスを巻き取り、息を吹き込み空洞をつくる	ガラスを3回巻きつけ、大きくする	4層目に粉ガラスをまぶし、熱して色をなじませる	息を吹き込みながら、かたちを整える	別途製作したパーツを熱し、ベースに熔着する	竿からガラスを切り離し、底面を整える
Roll glass around a blowpipe and blow into it to create a cavity.	Wrap around the glass three times to make it larger.	Sprinkle the fourth layer with beige powdered glass and heat to blend the color.	Shape the glass while blowing into it.	Heat the parts and fuse them onto the base.	Cut off the glass from the rod and shape the bottom.

模玉ガラス
異なる色のガラスを練り合わせ、琥珀や瑪瑙などの天然素材に近づけた。

Jade glass
A glass material that is made to resemble natural materials such as amber, agate, and marble.

ヴュラージュ
ガラス内部に気泡を封入する技法を再現。

Air bubbles inclusion
A technique of sealing air bubbles in glass.

ペルル・メタリック
ガラス器の表面に金や銀、プラチナの箔を挟み込む技法を再現。

Metal foil inclusion
A technique of fusing gold, silver and platinum foil onto the glass surface and sandwiching it between transparent or colored glass layers.

Simose Art Museum

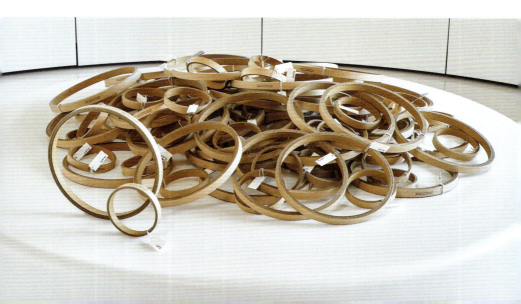

SIMOSE オリジナルグッズ　坂 茂の紙管

Simose Art Garden Villaの「紙の家」をはじめ、施設建築やインテリアに用いられている再生紙の紙管。坂 茂の象徴ともいえるこの素材をコンパクトなオブジェに仕立てました。

SIMOSE Original Goods: Shigeru Ban's Paper Tubes

Paper tubes, a building material used in the "Paper House" and other parts of the buildings and furniture in the SIMOSE complex, are made into art objects. This signature material of Shigeru Ban has been transformed into compact objects d'art.

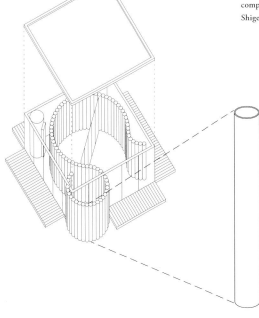

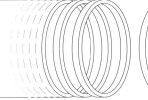

大小2種類の紙管を、それぞれ2cm間隔で輪切りにして販売。
Two different sized paper tubes, one large and one small, are each sliced into 2 cm-thick rings for sale.

Simose Art Museum

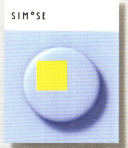

可動展示室の多彩なキューブをモチーフに、オリジナルグラフィックを展開。エミール・ガレの庭から着想した軍手(写真上)、日常に寄り添うマグネット(写真下)などさまざまなグッズを揃えています。

Original graphics are developed using the motif of the colorful cubes of the movable galleries. Various goods are available, including work gloves inspired by the Emile Gallé's garden (top photo) and magnets (bottom photo) for daily use.

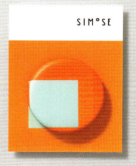

Dialogue I　アート施設とクリエイション
Art Facilities and Creation

坂 茂　　原 研哉
Shigeru BAN　　Kenya HARA

愉楽の時間にアートを挿入する

坂　　はじまりは、広島で建築金物を製造販売する企業のオーナーから私立美術館の設計を依頼されたことに遡ります。もともと広島市内に敷地を計画していたのですが、予定地が美術館建設に適切でないことが分かり、他の候補地を探すことになったんです。そうしたところ大竹市に、瀬戸内海に350mほど面する素晴らしい土地があって。けれど4.6haという面積は単体の美術館としては広すぎることや、市内から離れていることから、美術館だけでなくもう少しわざわざ来たくなる魅力が欲しいと思い、僕からオーベルジュを併設しようと提案しました。

原　　大竹市は巨大な石油化学コンビナートを擁する町で文化施設には恵まれていませんでしたが、海辺に忽然とアート複合施設ができたわけですから、広島の人たちも含めてちょっと意表を突かれたのではないでしょうか。

坂　　海外に行くと、きれいな海辺には必ずそれを享受するためのホテルやレストランがありますが、日本の海辺は工場になっていたり、ほとんど使われていなかったりすることが多い。こんなに美しい海景に囲まれているのだから、もっとそれを満喫できる宿泊施設やレストランがあるべきだと思ったんです。

原　　あったとしても、景色を独占するようなビルがそびえ立っている。

坂　　70年代から80年代の開発で海や湖の近くにできた建物は、軒並み高層ですよね。

原　　そうですね。けれど大切なのはどうやって風土とか、環境とか、風景を咀嚼するかだと思うんです。もしも建築がなかったら、その土地の魅力が分からなかったかもしれない、という空間をどうつくるか、ではないでしょうか。

坂　　その話で言うと、これまでは建物単体をデザインし、建物と敷地の隙間をランドスケープアーキテクトに埋めてもらうことがほとんどでしたが、今回はとにかく土地そのものが広大で素晴らしいので、ランドスケープの中に建築をどうつくるか、という逆の視点で設計を進めていきました。これまでやったこ

Inject Art into an Enjoyable Time

Ban   It all started when the owner of a company that manufactures and sells architectural hardware in Hiroshima asked me to design a private art museum. We had originally started our plans on a project site in Hiroshima City, but we found that the proposed site was not suitable for the construction of an art museum, and decided to look for other potential sites. Then, we found a wonderful site along the coastline of Otake City, facing 350 meters along the Seto Inland Sea. However, given that the 4.6 hectare site was too large for a stand-alone museum and that it was far from the city, I thought we needed to offer something more appealing that would entice visitors to come all the way to the area, so I proposed adding an auberge to the museum.

Hara   Otake City has a huge petrochemical complex, but because the city lacked cultural facilities, the sudden appearance of this art complex on the seaside must have taken the locals and the rest of the people in Hiroshima by surprise.

Ban   When I go abroad, I always find beautiful beaches with hotels and restaurants which can be enjoyed by many people. On the other hand, Japanese beaches are often industrialized or barely used. Since we are surrounded by beautiful seascapes like this, I thought we should have more accommodations and restaurants to enjoy them to the fullest.

Hara   Even if such facilities are available, they are often towering buildings that monopolize the view.

Ban   Buildings built on or near the sea or lakes during the development of the 70s and 80s were mostly high-rise.

Hara   Right. However, what is important is how we appreciate the climate, the environment, and the landscape and create spaces that make one think if it were not for this architecture, the allure of this area may never have been discovered.

とがないプロセスなので楽しかったですね。

原　夜明け前に建築を眺めると、美術館の壁面に海と空が映っていて、建築そのものが見えなくなっていくような不思議な感覚になりました。あの建物はどのように構想されたのでしょうか。

坂　瀬戸内海に沿った美しい敷地ではあるのですが、実は裏手がショッピングセンターに面していて、ちょっと俗っぽい感じがあるなと。それに、美術館のホワイトキューブや管理棟、収蔵庫といったボリュームのある建物をそのまま屹立させると、せっかくの風景が台無しになると思ったんです。そこで、長さ180m、高さ8.5mのミラーガラスの壁を立てて、存在感のある建物を視界から隠しつつ周囲の景色を増幅させる仕組みを考えました。

原　可動展示棟の方はカラフルなキューブになっていますが、それが海に浮かんでいるようで、瀬戸内の島々を象徴しているようで面白い建築ですよね。

坂　浮かせる、というアイデアは昔から温めていたのですが、敷地内から瀬戸内海の島々を眺めることで具現化されていきました。建築というのは不動産という言葉の通り動かないものですが、季節やオケージョンによって動いたり変化したりする建築があってもいいのではないかとずっと考えていたんです。原さんが企画されたHOUSE VISION 2に出展した「凝縮と開放の家」では、壁と屋根がジッパーで着脱でき、着替えられる建築を提案しましたし、ヴィジュアル・アイデンティティを構築していただいたパリのラ・セーヌ・ミュージカル

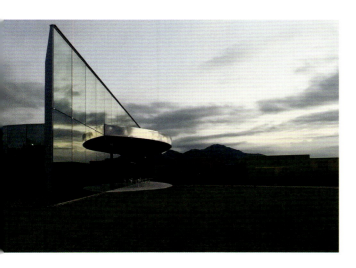

Ban Speaking of which, in the past, we as architects would design buildings only and let landscape architects fill in the gaps between the buildings and the site in most cases. But for this project, since the land itself was so vast and wonderful, we proceeded with the design from the opposite perspective, that is, creating architecture in the landscape.

Hara When I looked at the museum before dawn, I had an extraordinary sensation of seeing the reflection of the sea and the sky on the walls, as if the architecture itself was disappearing from view. How did you conceive of the building?

Ban While it is a beautiful site along the Seto Inland Sea, it faces a shopping center in the back, which seemed somewhat mundane. Besides, I thought that voluminous buildings such as museum's "white cube" spaces, administrative wing, and storage building, soaring over the landscape would spoil the scenery. Therefore, we came up with a mechanism to amplify the surrounding scenery while hiding the building's presence from view by erecting a 180-meter-long, 8.5-meter-high mirrored glass wall.

Hara The movable exhibition buildings are colorful cubes that seem to float in the sea. They are also interesting architecture because they appear to symbolize the islands of the Seto Inland Sea.

可動展示棟の施工時、海上から台船を搬入する様子

では太陽が動くことで形態が変わる建築をつくったのですが、そういった建築に可動性や開放性を持たせたいという考えがSIMOSEで結実したんです。造船技術が発達している広島だからこそ実現できたもので、一棟ずつ台船工場でつくって、船で引っ張って敷地まで運搬してきました。

原　　空間に可変性があるので、展示も割とおおらかなことができるのではないでしょうか。美術館や博物館というと情報がぎっしり詰め込まれていて、それを観て堪能しないといけない、といったイメージを持たれがちですよね。もっとゆったりとした空間の中で、ご飯を食べて、景色を眺めて、コーヒーを飲んで、ついでにアートも観て、というぐらいの、愉楽の時間にアートを挿入するというようなバランスがちょうどいいのかもしれません。

屹立する建築、ならしていくデザイン

坂　　SIMOSEは結果的に複合的な機能を持つ施設になりましたが、コミュニケーションデザインはどのようにお考えになられたのでしょうか。

原　　今回は坂さんの耕したものが既にあったので、僕は施設のネーミングやヴィジュアル・アイデンティティ、サイン計画などをとおして複合施設ならではの複雑さを明快に交通整理しつつ、どうしたらこの施設がより多くの人の目に届

Ban   The idea of floating buildings had long been on my mind, but it materialized as I observed the islands of the Seto Inland Sea from the site. The Japanese word for real estate is "fudosan," meaning "immovable assets." As it implies, architecture is something that does not move, but I have always thought that we could also have an architecture that moves and changes with the seasons and occasions. In the "House of Condensation and Openness," which we exhibited at the HOUSE VISION 2 exhibition that you organized, we proposed an architecture with walls and a roof that could be detached and reattached with zippers. And for La Seine Musicale in Paris, for which you developed a visual identity, we created an architecture that changed its form as the sun moved. Our idea of giving architecture such mobility and openness culminated with SIMOSE. It was made possible thanks to Hiroshima's advanced shipbuilding technology. The buildings were built one by one at a barge factory and towed by boat to the site.

Hara   The flexibility of the space allows for more freedom for exhibitions. People are often under the impression that art galleries and museums are packed with information that must be viewed and enjoyed. By injecting art into enjoyable activities such as admiring the scenery and drinking coffee, we can perhaps balance art and leisure so that viewers can appreciate art in a relaxing atmosphere.

Soaring Architecture,
Design to Shape Things the Way They Are Meant to Be

Ban   SIMOSE has become a mixed-use facility in the end. How did you approach the communication design?

Hara   This time, you had already plowed the field before I started. So, we considered how to make this facility more accessible to a wider audience and more pleasant to experience, while clearly organizing the complexity associated with a mixed-use facility through its naming, visual identity, and signage plan. As for the signage plan, given the vastness of the site and the size of the individual structures, we aimed for an information design that would counter the soaring architecture because discreet signage would go unnoticed. We call it "ant sign" because of their ant-like forms. They are designed to be

Dialogue I

くか、気持ちよく味わってもらえるかといったことを考えていました。サイン計画に関しては、敷地が広大でそれぞれの構造物も大きいので、さりげなく誘導しても気づかれないと思い、屹立する建築に拮抗する情報の形をデザインしています。アリのようなフォルムをしているので「アントサイン」と呼んでいるのですが、細い脚で自立してしっかりとしたボリュームがあり、とにかくそこに行けば情報がはっきり分かるという存在感を意識してデザインしています。

坂　　名前をつけるのも難しかったのではないでしょうか。オーナーの下瀬さんのローマ字表記からHをとった「SIMOSE」、これは覚えやすいですし、ロゴとしての強さもありますよね。

原　　随分とさまざまな名称案を練っていたのですが、やっぱり基幹となるのは個人コレクションですから、オーナーの名前を冠するのが相応しいなと。何かの頭文字なのか、フランス語なのかといった不思議な響きも感じられていいなと思ったんです。

坂　　グラフィックだけにとどまらず企業の戦略をつくったり、美術館や展覧会の方向性を出したりと、原さんは領域を問わずに活動する総合プロデューサーのようなデザイナーではないかと思います。

原　　坂さんとはある意味、芸風が違うんですよね。坂さんはラグビータイプというか、フォワードでぐいぐい突破していくような。僕はそれを、せっせと分かりやすく編集していく感じというか。

坂　　僕が他の建築家といちばん違うところは、構造から設計することだと思います。学生時代から、時代の趨勢に流されない建築家になりたいと考えていたのですが、アメリカのバックミンスター・フラーやドイツのフライ・オットーなど独自のスタイルを持っている建築家はみな、自分だけの構造方式や構法、素材を編み出しているという事実に気づいたんです。それから僕もずっと構造の設計から始めて、ジョイントや材料の設計などすべて自分でやるようにしています。原さんも終始自分でやるタイプですよね。

原　　そうですね。ですが僕の理想は、自分のデザインがどこにあるか分から

freestanding with thin legs and have a solid and voluminous presence, making the information clearly visible whenever you go up to them at any rate.

Ban   I guess naming the museum must have been a challenge. The name "SIMOSE" - taking out the H from the owner Yumiko Shimose's name - is easy to remember, and makes for an impactful logo, too.

Hara   We actually came up with many different names. But since this museum's mainstay is a private collection, we thought it would be appropriate to name it after the owner. We also liked this name because it had a mysterious ring to it, as if it were some kind of abbreviation or a French word.

Ban   I think you are a designer working across multiple fields, not only in graphics but also in creating corporate strategies, setting directions for museums and exhibitions, etc. I think of you as an all-round producer.

Hara   I think your artistic approach is different from mine, Mr. Ban. You are like a rugby player, a forward who pushes hard to break through. Whereas I work diligently to edit the material in a way that is easy to understand.

Ban   I think what sets me apart from other architects is that I start designing from the structure. Ever since I was a student, I wanted to become an architect who would never get carried away by the trends of the times. And I realized that architects who have their distinctive styles, such as Buckminster Fuller in the U.S. and Frei Otto in Germany, have developed their unique structural systems, methods, and materials. Since then, I started designing from the structure, and I try to design everything on my own, down to the joints and materials. You are also a Do-It-Myself type of person from start to finish, Mr. Hara.

Hara   You could say that. But ideally, I want my design to blend in so well that people don't even recognize its presence. The city you see outside your window and the table in front of you did not assume their shapes because some amazing designer created stunning designs but because they have taken on that shape. Such "things that became what they are" must possess absolute strength. Perhaps my artistic approach is to shape things as they were meant to be. Perhaps this project involves the works of two individuals: Shigeru Ban, who works with his soaring structure, and Kenya Hara, who works to shape

Dialogue I

ないくらい、こなれた状態になることを考えています。窓の外に見える町も、目の前にあるテーブルも、凄腕のデザイナーが目を奪うようなデザインをしたから形が定まったのではなくて、だんだんその形になってきたわけですよね。そういう「なってきたもの」の絶対的な強さがあるはずで。なるべくしてなってきたもののように形を整えていくのが僕の芸風なのかもしれません。屹立する構造の坂 茂、ならしていく原研哉という二人で仕事をしているのかもしれませんね。

坂　下瀬美術館でも、アート作品だけでなく建築やデザインの展覧会があるといいですよね。デンマークのルイジアナ近代美術館のような、ギャラリーを回ってちょっと海を見て戻ってくるという楽しみ方ができる場所なので、展示も都市の美術館にはない企画が見られるといいなと思います。

原　広島市街から車で40分程度と、都市とはほどよい離れ方をしているところもルイジアナ近代美術館と似ています。僕らの仕事はこれから少しずつ役割を果たしていくことになると思います。施設自体ある意味ではようやく骨格ができたというところなので、これからどういう施設に育っていくのかに注目したいですね。アート空間でアートを満喫するだけでも、宿泊をして建築的愉楽がいかなるものかを経験する上でも、この施設がより多くの人々と出会うことを願っています。

things the way they are meant to be.

Ban   It would be great to see exhibitions of architecture and design as well as of artwork at the Simose Art Museum. Since the place offers the experience of going around the galleries, looking at the sea for a while, and then coming back, like the Louisiana Museum of Modern Art in Denmark, I hope to see exhibitions and projects that visitors do not experience in urban art museums.

Hara   It is also similar to the Louisiana Museum of Modern Art in that it is about 40 minutes' drive from downtown Hiroshima, which is a good distance from the city. I think our work will gradually start fulfilling its role from now on. In a sense, the facility has finally established its framework, and I am looking forward to seeing what kind of facility it will develop into in the future. I hope this facility will receive a wider range of visitors, whether they are here just to enjoy the art in the art space or stay overnight and experience the architectural pleasures of the place.

サインシステム

Signage System

複合施設であるSIMOSEを迷うことなく誘導・案内するために設計された「アントサイン」。黒い円盤から細長い脚がのびたデザインは、広大な敷地を回遊する体験を盛り立てます。大小さまざまな円盤を上下左右に連ねることで、順路、設備、施設名称など必要な情報をふさわしい順番で伝えられるよう工夫されています。

"Ant Signs" were designed to guide visitors through the SIMOSE complex. The design with long, slender legs extending out from the black disks enhances the visitors' experience of walking around the vast grounds. Disks of various sizes are arranged both vertically and horizontally to convey the necessary information in the proper order, such as routes, available amenities, and facility names.

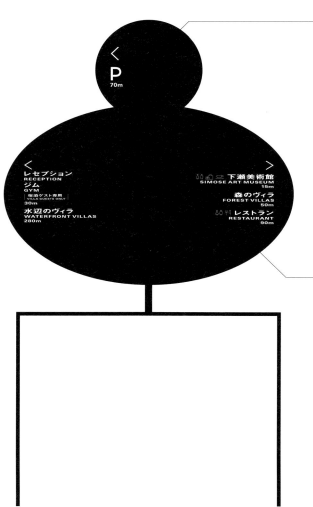

順路を示す矢印、場所を示すピクトグラムの順に表示して、どこに何があるかを表示しています。
The sign indicates "where and what is ahead" with arrows indicating the directions and then pictograms depicting types of facilities.

下部の大きな円盤では、施設名称や注意事項、図など詳細なインフォメーションを表示。人の目線に自然と入るよう傾斜が付けられています。
The large disk at the bottom displays detailed information consisting of facility names, notices, and diagrams. It is tilted at an angle so that it naturally falls into one's line of sight.

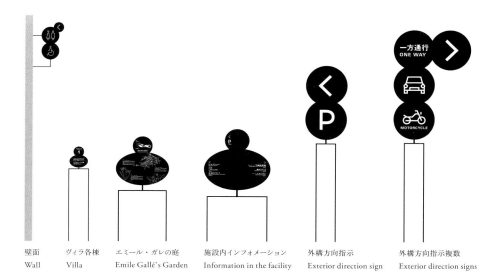

壁面	ヴィラ各棟	エミール・ガレの庭	施設内インフォメーション	外構方向指示	外構方向指示複数
Wall	Villa	Emile Gallé's Garden	Information in the facility	Exterior direction sign	Exterior direction signs

屋内のあちこちに顔を覗かせる壁付けサイン、主に屋外に点在する自立式サインの2種を展開。設置する場所と、掲載する情報の量に合わせて円盤の大きさや高さが調節されています。

Two types of signs are available: wall-mounted signs that peek out here and there indoors, and freestanding signs that are mainly scattered outdoors. The size and height of the disks are adjusted to suit the location and the amount of information to be posted.

エミール・ガレの庭に立つ案内サイン（一部）。大きな円盤をキャンバスのように使い、代表的な植物をテキストと線画イラストで紹介しています。

A guide sign (partial view) standing in Emile Gallé's Garden. This large disk is used as a canvas to introduce some representative plants with text and line illustrations.

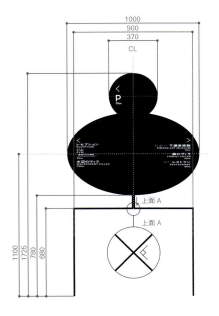

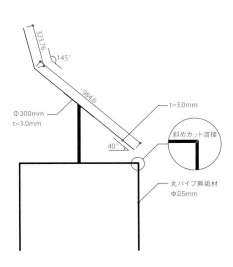

Simose Art Garden Villa

広大な敷地にたたずむ10棟のヴィラをはじめ、地元の幸を生かしたフレンチレストラン、下瀬美術館や庭園の散策などが楽しめるアート・オーベルジュです。海岸線の南と北に配された「森のヴィラ」と「水辺のヴィラ」という2つのエリアに、坂 茂の初期の実験住宅からこの地のための新作まで個性豊かなヴィラが点在。現代建築に暮らすように滞在しながら、瀬戸内の自然を存分に享受する新しい体験が待っています。

Simose Art Garden Villa

Simose Art Garden Villa is an art auberge with 10 villas on a vast site, where visitors can enjoy a French restaurant featuring local delicacies, the Simose Art Museum, and a stroll through the garden. The two areas arranged on the north and south sides of the coastline, the "Forest Villa" and the "Waterfront Villa," are dotted with unique villas ranging from Shigeru Ban's early experimental houses to his new works designed for this site. Visitors will enjoy a new experience of staying in contemporary architectural works as if living in their homes while fully savoring the natural beauty of the Seto Inland Sea.

レセプション棟

旅のはじまりを木の香りで迎えるレセプション棟。宿泊者用フロントとして設計された、シンプルな切妻屋根の建築です。ひときわ目を惹く三角形の骨組みは、スギの板材を圧密化してL型に成形したもの。それらをボルトで接合し、トラス状の柱と梁を構成することで、鉄骨造のように繊細な架構を木造で実現しています。

Reception

The reception building welcomes guests with the scent of wood at the beginning of their journey. It is a simple gable-roofed building designed as a reception area for guests. The eye-catching triangular framework is made of compressed cedar planks formed into an L shape. These are bolted together to form a post-and-beam truss structure, achieving a wooden structure that is as delicate as a steel frame structure.

Scale=1/300

072 — 073

森のヴィラ

木立の合間に、全く趣の異なる5棟のヴィラが点在。坂 茂が初期に手掛けた、ケース・スタディ・ハウスといわれる実験的な住宅建築の代表作をヴィラとして再設計した4棟と、この地のために新たに設計された1棟で構成されています。

Forest Villas

Five villas with completely different characteristics are scattered among the trees. Four of the villas are redesigned from Shigeru Ban's early experimental case study houses, and one is newly designed for this site.

Villa 1　ダブル・ルーフの家
House of Double-Roof

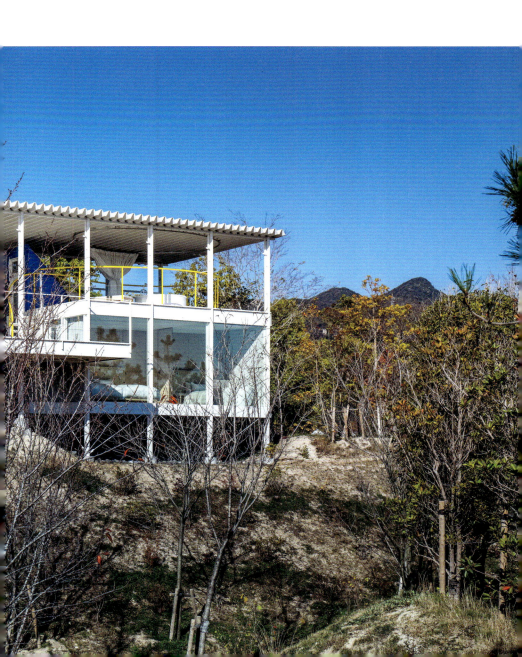

大きな屋根の下に複数の屋根を持つ「ダブル・ルーフの家」。1993年、山中湖の傾斜地に建てられた別荘を宿泊施設として再設計したものです。山中湖など積雪地帯の建築は、雪の重さに耐えるため大きな架構が必要とされますが、そのためだけに一年中必要な梁を大きくすることは形態、材料、コストの面でもったいないと坂 茂は考え、屋根と天井を切り離す二重屋根構造を提案。応力上、積雪荷重を受けられる最小サイズの折板屋根で全体を覆い、それとは別に天井の架構を独立させることで、躯体への影響を解消しました。意匠面ではスイス・チューリッヒにある「ル・コルビュジエ・センター」(1967)の影響を受けており、赤、黄、緑といったアクセントカラーはデ・ステイルに由来しています。

The House of Double-Roof has several small roofs under a grand roof. The villa, originally built on a sloping site in Lake Yamanaka in 1993, was redesigned as an accommodation facility. Architecture in snowy regions such as Lake Yamanaka requires large structures to withstand snow loads. However, Shigeru Ban thought that enlarging the beams only to support the snow load would be wasteful in terms of form, materials, and cost throughout the year, and proposed a double-roof structure that separates the roof from the ceilings. The entire structure is covered with corrugated roof of the minimum size to bear the snow load in terms of stress and separate the ceiling framing from it, thereby resolving its impact on the frame. The design was influenced by the "Le Corbusier Center" (1967) in Zurich, Switzerland, and the accent colors of red, yellow, and green are derived from De Stijl.

大屋根の下に設けたテラスを挟み、LDKと寝室・バスルームを配置。後者は地形に合わせて半階分下がっており、屋上に瀬戸内海を望むジャグジーバスが設けられています。

The LDK (living / dining / kitchen area) and the bedroom/bathroom are arranged across the terrace under the grand roof. The bedroom/bathroom is lowered by half a floor in keeping with the topography, and a jacuzzi overlooking the Seto Inland Sea is on the rooftop.

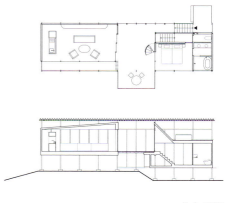

Scale=1/400

Simose Art Garden Villa

078 — 079

Villa 2　壁のない家
Wall-Less House

Simose Art Garden Villa

「壁のない家」は1997年、軽井沢の傾斜地に建てられた別荘を宿泊施設として再設計したものです。斜面に住宅をつくる場合、地面を平らにするために擁壁が必要となります。本作では基礎工事を軽減するため、斜面を掘って床面の後半分を下げ、掘った土を床面の前半分に盛ることで地面そのものを平らにつくりかえるとともに、斜面を掘った後辺に向かって床面を曲線状に屋根までめくり上げることで擁壁兼耐震壁とし、土圧をはじめすべての水平力を自然と床面に流しています。これにより室内は、直径わずか55㎜の柱が3本立つのみの空間となり、まるで天と地との間に浮かぶような暮らし方が生まれました。

The Wall-Less House, a villa originally built on a sloping site in Karuizawa in 1997, was redesigned as an accommodation facility. Retaining walls are required to level the ground when building a house on a slope. In this project, the ground was excavated to lower the rear half of the floor to reduce the amount of foundation work, and the excavated soil was used to fill the front half of the floor to level the ground. Then, the floor was turned up to the roof in a curvilinear shape toward the rear edge of the excavated slope to form a retaining and seismic wall, which naturally transfers earth pressure and other lateral forces to the floor surface. As a result, the interior space has only three pillars with diameters as small as 55 millimeters, creating a new lifestyle that seems to float between heaven and earth.

すべての壁をなくし、ガラスの引き戸でフレキシブルに仕切る「ユニバーサル・フロア」の考え方を実現。リビング、キッチン、バスルームなどが同一の床面に配されており、室内のどこにいても樹々、海、空とつながる浮遊感が楽しめます。

The concept of a "universal floor" is realized by eliminating all walls and dividing the space flexibly with sliding glass doors. The living room, kitchen, and bathroom are all located on the same floor, allowing residents to enjoy a floating sensation of being connected to the trees, sea, and sky from anywhere in the room.

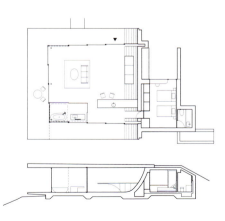

Scale=1/400

Simose Art Garden Villa

Villa 3　十字壁の家
　　　　　Cross Wall House

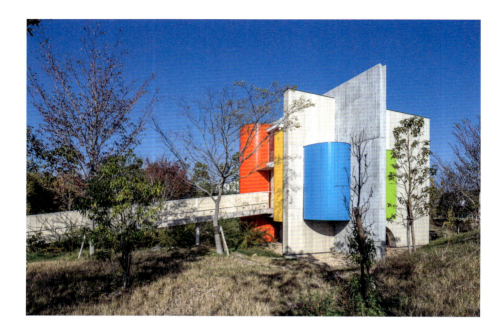

2枚の壁を十字に組み合わせた「十字壁の家」。Simose Art Garden Villaのために新たに設計されました。RCの壁そのものを支柱としながら、その壁面に地面から浮かせる形で居住空間のボリュームを取り付けています。エントランスはピロティ状に持ち上げられており、スロープでアプローチします。本作は、ケース・スタディ・ハウスに取り組みはじめた初期の思想に立ち返り、かつて坂 茂が学んだクーパーユニオン建築学科の学科長であり大きな影響を受けたというジョン・ヘイダックへのオマージュとしてデザインされました。水平線、垂直線が際立つ造形や三原色を取り入れた表現は、ヘイダックの作品に見られるデ・ステイルの考え方を取り入れたものだといいます。

The Cross Wall House, which combines two walls in a crisscross pattern, was newly designed for the Simose Art Garden Villa. The reinforced concrete walls serve as the supporting pillar, and the living space volume is attached to them in a way that it floats above the ground. The entrance is raised to form a pilotis, and is approached via a ramp. The project goes back to Shigeru Ban's early ideas about case study houses and was designed as a homage to John Hejduk, the head of the architecture department at Cooper Union, where Shigeru Ban studied and who was a major influence on him. The design of the building, with its prominent horizontal and vertical lines and the use of three primary colors is said to have been inspired by the De Stijl concept found in Hejduk's works.

十字壁の内側にはベッドルームを配置。十字壁の外側には、クローゼットやシャワールーム、トイレ、階段、各設備がそれぞれ独立したボリュームとして取り付けられています。3階には檜風呂のあるバスリビングがあり、瀬戸内の海景を一望できます。

Bedrooms are located inside the cross walls. A closet, shower room, toilet, staircase, and other facilities are installed on the outside of those walls as separate volumes. On the third floor, there is a living room-like bathing space with a hinoki cypress bathtub, offering a panoramic view of the Seto Inland Sea.

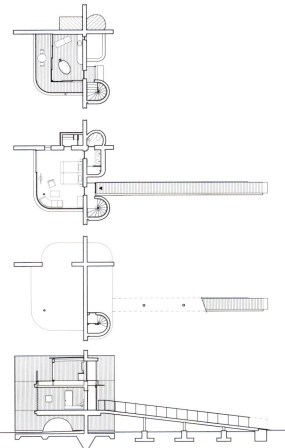

Scale=1/400

Simose Art Garden Villa

Villa 4　家具の家
Furniture House

「家具の家」は1995年、山中湖に建てられた別荘を宿泊施設として再設計したものです。地震のときに家具と家具の間にいたために落ちてくる屋根から身を守ることができたという人々の話から、本棚やクローゼットなど家具の強度に着目し、そこに屋根をかければ空間ができるという発想に至りました。家具そのものを、家を支える構造体にすることで、壁も柱もないすっきりとした空間を実現。内外壁の塗装などすべて工場で行うため、資源や現場での作業量、工費などいっさい無駄なく仕立てられています。既存の材料の意味や機能を置き換えることで、すべてにおいて合理的でバランスのよい建築が生まれました。

The Furniture House, a villa originally built on Lake Yamanaka in 1995, was redesigned as an accommodation facility. This work was inspired by people's accounts about how they managed to protect themselves from falling roofs by staying between pieces of furniture during earthquakes. Shigeru Ban focused on the strength of furniture pieces such as bookshelves and closets and conceived the idea of creating a space by putting a roof over them. By using the furniture as a structure that supports the house, an unobstructed space without walls or pillars was achieved. All work, including interior and exterior wall painting, was carried out in the factory, so no waste of resources, on-site workload, or labor costs occurred during the construction. By giving new meanings and functions to existing materials, an architecture that is rational and well-balanced in every way was created.

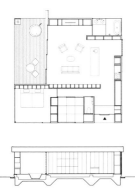

Scale=1/400

Simose Art Garden Villa

Villa 5　紙の家
Paper House

Simose Art Garden Villa

再生紙の紙管を用いた「紙の家」。1995年、山中湖に建てられた別荘を宿泊施設として再設計したものです。10×10mの床に110本の紙管をS字状に並べ、正方形と円弧の内外に多様な空間を形成しています。80本の紙管で構成される大きな円弧の内側に居住空間、外側に回廊があり、回廊に独立する直径123cmの紙管にはトイレを内包。並んだ紙管は風雨を遮ると同時に柔らかな光を室内に取り込みます。このような紙の建築が発想されたきっかけは、1986年、アルヴァ・アアルト展の会場設計をした頃に遡ります。予算の制約と会期後の解体を念頭におきながらアアルトを想起させる建築空間を考えていたところ、ファブリックの芯として使われていた紙管に目が留まり、木の代用としたのです。のちに構造研究を重ねて耐水や耐火、強度といった問題を解決、実証。いまや坂建築を象徴する建材として、災害時の仮設住宅から恒久的な公共施設まで国内外で用いられています。

The Paper House made of recycled paper tubes, originally a villa built on Lake Yamanaka in 1995, was redesigned as an accommodation facility. One hundred and ten paper tubes are arranged in an S-shape on a 10 by 10 meter floor, forming various spaces inside and outside of the square and arc. A large arc composed of 80 paper tubes contains a living space inside and a corridor outside. A toilet is enclosed in a 123-centimeter-diameter paper tube that stands alone in the corridor. These arranged paper tubes block out the wind and rain, while simultaneously letting gentle light into the room. This idea of paper architecture dates back to 1986, when Shigeru Ban designed the venue for the Alvar Aalto exhibition. While thinking of an architectural space evocative of Aalto's work, with budget constraints and dismantling of the building after the exhibition in mind, the paper tubes used for fabric rolls caught Ban's attention and decided to use them instead of wood. Later, he conducted a series of structural studies to resolve the problems of water, fire, and strength, and verified the results. Today, paper tubes are a signature material of Ban's architecture, and are used in Japan and abroad for many purposes, from temporary housing in disaster areas to permanent public facilities.

紙管で構成された大きな円弧の内側には、居住空間が広がります。独立したキッチンカウンター、引き戸、可動式クローゼットのみが点在するユニバーサル・フロアです。また、小さな円弧は浴室と坪庭を囲い込んでおり、外部の紙管は目隠しスクリーンとして自立しています。

The living space inside a larger arc composed of paper tubes is a universal floor interspersed only with a separate kitchen counter, sliding doors, and movable closets. A small arc encloses the bathroom and tsuboniwa (courtyard garden) while the external paper tubes are freestanding and serve as blindfold screens.

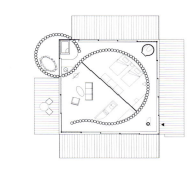

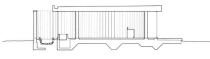

Scale=1/400

外周部のガラスの引き戸を開け放つと、紙管の列柱に支持された水平な屋根が強調され、回廊とテラスが連続します。

Opening the sliding glass doors around the perimeter emphasizes the horizontal roof supported by rows of paper tube columns and links the corridor to the terrace.

Simose Art Garden Villa

ファブリックはすべてテキスタイルデザイナーの須藤玲子によるもの。空間に可変性を与える存在として坂 茂はヴィラ内のカーテンに着目、対して須藤はヴィラごとの建築や眺望に応じて異なる意匠のファブリックをあつらえました。写真左は「壁のない家」のカーテンで、宮島や背後の山々に見られる「尾根」がモチーフです。

All fabrics have been made by textile designer Reiko Sudo. Shigeru Ban focused on how the curtains can give more flexibility to the spaces, whereas Sudo has created fabrics with different designs in response to the architecture and vistas from each villa. The left photo shows the curtain of the "House without Walls," featuring the "ridge" motif of Miyajima Island and the mountains behind it.

部屋の家具も坂 茂によるオリジナル。写真下は、単一のL型ユニットを繰り返し使い、椅子やテーブルを構成する「L-ユニット システム」で展開されたチェアです。組み立てるための接合部として開けられた穴が独自の表情をもたらしています。

The furniture pieces in the room are also Shigeru Ban's original designs. The chair in the lower photo was developed using the "L-unit system," in which an L-shaped unit is used repeatedly to form chairs and tables. The holes drilled for joints lend the piece a unique expression.

Simose Art Garden Villa

水辺のヴィラ

海沿いに広がる水盤に面して、5棟のヴィラが連立しています。キールステックという構造用パネルを合理的かつ意匠的に使用した、この地のための新しい建築です。連泊や再訪の楽しみづくりとして、すべて異なる内装にデザインされています。

Waterfront Villas

A series of five villas face a water feature that stretches along the sea. A building structural material called Kielsteg is used in a rational yet aesthetic way to create a new architecture for this site. Every room is designed with a different interior to create an enjoyable experience for guests staying multiple nights or returning.

Villa 6-10 キールステックの家 A−E
Kielsteg House A−E

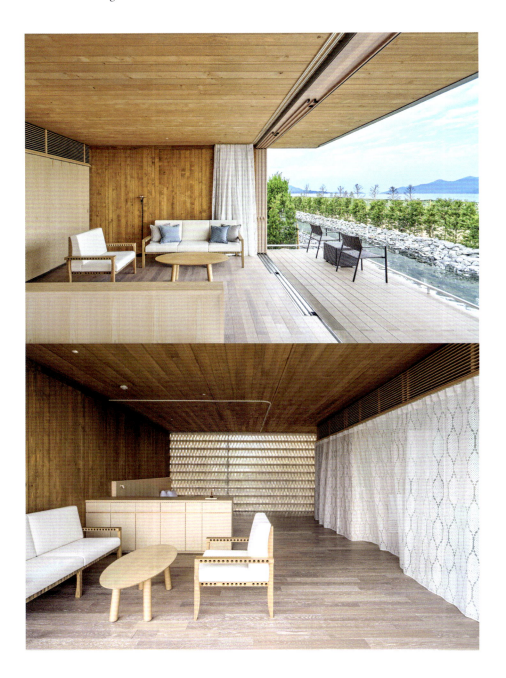

Simose Art Garden Villa

水辺のヴィラを設計するにあたり、坂 茂が採用したのはオーストリア生まれの木製ストレストスキンパネル「Kielsteg（キールステック）」を多方面に使った構法でした。船を支える竜骨（キール）のような特徴的な断面を持つことからその名が付いた、軽量かつ高性能な建築部材です。本来は床や屋根に用いられるこの材を、壁としても利用。さらに、短く切って積み上げることで普段は見られない断面の美しさを露呈させながら、室内に柔らかな光を取り込むルーバーとしての機能も持たせています。5棟のヴィラはすべて異なる内装となっており、和室タイプ、洋室タイプをはじめ、引き戸やカーテンで空間を仕切ったり家具の配置を変えたりと、さまざまな工夫が凝らされています。

In designing the Waterfront Villas, Shigeru Ban adopted a construction method that uses "Kielsteg," a wooden stressed skin panel from Austria, in multiple ways. This lightweight, high-performance building material was named for its distinctive cross-section, which resembles the keel that supports a ship. Originally used for floors and roofs, it was adopted to form the walls for this project. The material is cut into short pieces and stacked to expose the beauty of the cross-section, which is not normally seen, while also functioning as louvers to let soft light into the rooms. All five villas are furnished differently, ranging from Japanese-style to Western-style rooms, dividing the space with sliding doors and curtains, and arranging the furniture in different ways.

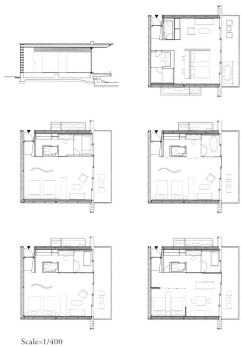

Scale=1/400

Simose Art Garden Villa

ヴィラの備品・アメニティのデザイン。SIMOSEオリジナルグッズと同じく可動展示室に着想を得たグラフィックで展開されています。部屋においたときの馴染みの良さを考慮し、ニュートラルなシルバーカラーが採用されました。

The designs of the villa's fixtures and amenities feature graphics inspired by the movable galleries like SIMOSE's original goods. A neutral silver color was adopted to harmonize with the rooms in which fixtures and amenities are placed.

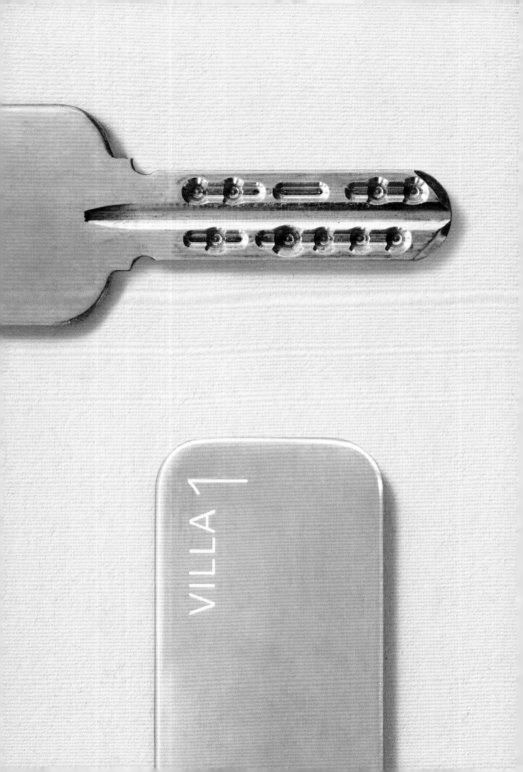

宿泊する棟の線画をあしらった、門を開けるカードキー。精緻な金属加工で穏やかな丸みを削り出した、家を開けるディンプルキー。2つのカギをぴったりと収める革製のキーケース。ヴィラに出入りする瞬間から高揚感を掻き立てるため、カギのデザインにも工夫が凝らされています。

The card key that opens the gate features a line drawing of the building where the guest will stay. The dimple key to the house has been precisely machined to create gentle, round dimples, and the leather key case holds the two keys perfectly. The keys are ingeniously designed to spark a sense of excitement from the moment you enter the villa.

Simose Art Garden Villa

SIMOSE French Restaurant

広島近郊で育った肉や魚介、有機野菜、柑橘など季節ごとの食材を吟味して、その本来の味や香りを生かした一皿に仕立てます。動物性脂肪を控えた料理は、食べ飽きにくくもたれにくい軽やかさが魅力です。オープンキッチンでシェフが腕をふるう音を聴き、刻々とうつろう瀬戸内海を眺めながら、地元の幸をゆったりとお召し上がりいただけます。

SIMOSE French Restaurant

Meat, seafood, organic vegetables, citrus fruits, and other seasonal ingredients grown in the vicinity of Hiroshima are carefully selected and prepared into dishes that bring out their genuine flavors and aromas. The dishes are low in animal fat, making them appealing and light. Guests will enjoy a leisurely meal of local delicacies while listening to the sound of the chefs at work in the open kitchen and gazing out at the ever-changing Seto Inland Sea.

ライブ感あふれるオープンキッチン。一般的に厨房は背丈ほどある冷蔵庫や排気フードなどで視線を遮られてしまいますが、排気フード以外をカウンターの高さに抑えることで、周囲のランドスケープに集中できるようになっています。

This open kitchen is full of a lively atmosphere. While kitchens are generally blocked from view by tall refrigerators and ventilation hoods, this kitchen keeps everything except the ventilation hoods at counter height, allowing diners to concentrate on enjoying the surrounding landscape.

料理を手掛ける久重浩シェフは、かつて東京・白金台の「OZAWA」を率いたフレンチの巨匠、小沢貴彦の思想と技術を継承。地元を中心に生産者を訪ねて食材を厳選し、その味と香りを最大限に活かした料理を生み出しています。器を彩るハーブは、敷地内の庭で育てられたものです。

Chef Hiroshi Hisashige inherited the philosophy and techniques of master French chef Takahiko Ozawa, who once headed OZAWA, a French restaurant in Shirokanedai, Tokyo. He carefully selects ingredients by visiting mainly local producers and creates dishes that make the most of their flavors and aromas. The herbs that embellish the dishes are grown in the garden on the premises.

SIMOSE French Restaurant

風景の中に屋根をおく

人にとっての気持ちのいい空間とは、外と内の中間的な領域であると坂 茂は考えています。レストランもまた食を味わうかたわらで景色や光、陰影、風を楽しみ、皆で語り合う場とするために、ランドスケープの中に屋根をおいただけのような建築を設計。屋根の中央に鉄骨とヒノキ集成材でできた梁を十字に架け、その中をヒノキ集成材の梁で分割し、それらを外周のサッシで支えながら水平力を暖炉とトイレの壁で受けることで、開放的で内部にも外部にもなる空間を実現しています。

Putting a Roof over the Landscape

Shigeru Ban believes that the most pleasant space for people is an intermediate area between the outside and inside. This restaurant was designed as if a roof was placed in the landscape to provide a place where people can enjoy the scenery, light, shade, and wind and talk with each other while savoring the food. Steel and laminated hinoki cypress beams span the center of the roof in a crisscross pattern. These beams are divided by laminated cypress beams, which are supported by mullions around the perimeter. The fireplace and toilet walls bear horizontal forces, creating an open space that can be both inside and outside.

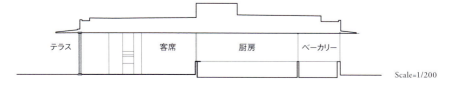

Scale=1/200

SIMOSE French Restaurant

ワインリストとメニュー表は、テーブルクロスなどにも用いられる黄色と、瀬戸内海の明るいブルーをそれぞれ配し、空間のアクセントとして心地よく機能させています。伝票ケースのファブリックデザインは、須藤玲子によるものです。

The wine list and menu chart are designed to accentuate the space with the yellow color used for tablecloths and the bright blue of the Seto Inland Sea, respectively. Reiko Sudo designed the fabric for the slipcase.

Menu du Diner

ディナーメニュー

最初のひとくち
Amuse-Bouche

広島野菜の小さなスープ
Petite Soupe de Légumes

A. オードヴル
Les Entrées

車海老とトマトのゼリー寄せ 赤ピーマンのソース
Gelée de crevettes et tomate servi avec sauce aux poivrons rouges

鯛の昆布じめ 山芋のパンケーキとキャヴィア
Daurade crue parfumée aux algues sur une crêpe au caviar

B. 温かいオードヴル
Les Entrées chaudes

地卵のココット トリュフのソース
Œuf cocotte avec sauce aux truffes

白アスパラガスの茹でたて蛤のソース レモンタイム
Asperges Blanches Chaudes,
Sauce palourdes au thym citron

Dialogue II ヴィラ建築と瀬戸内海
Villa Architecture and Seto Inland Sea

坂 茂　×　原 研哉
Shigeru BAN　　Kenya HARA

訪れるたびに、新しい発見を

原　美術館やレストラン、そして10棟のヴィラと、これだけの建築を一手に設計できるとは、建築家冥利につきるのではないでしょうか。おひなさまやエミール・ガレといったコレクションのための美術館を持つと同時に、施設全体が坂 茂の建築ミュージアムになっていることがSIMOSEの大きな特徴だと思います。

坂　今回のプロジェクトは、稀に見る全面的なクライアントの理解とサポートがあってこそのものだと思っています。ヴィラについては30代の頃、実験的な材料や構法を用いて毎回違うテーマで個人住宅をつくる「ケース・スタディ・ハウス」という試みをしていたのですが、いま振り返ってもよくつくったなと思っていまして。住んでいる人以外に見ていただけないことをもったいなく感じるほどでした。そんなときにSIMOSEの話をいただいて、この敷地にちょうどいい大きさだったものですから、再設計のご提案をしたら受け入れていただいたという経緯です。

Every Visit Brings a New Discovery

Hara   It must have been a great privilege for an architect to design so many buildings at once, including a museum, restaurant, and ten villas. I think SIMOSE's significant features include the fact that it has dedicated museums for collections such as Ohinasama (a set of traditional ornamental dolls modeled after the Imperial Court of the Heian period, displayed on the Girls' Day) and Emile Gallé, and also that the entire facility serves as Shigeru Ban's architectural museum.

Ban   This project was made possible thanks to the exceptional and wholehearted understanding and support of the client. The villa design is based on experimental Case Study Houses I realized in my 30s, using experimental materials and construction methods to build private homes with a different theme each time. Looking back on it, I was convinced we had done an excellent job but felt it was a shame that only the people who lived in the houses were able to appreciate them. While I was thinking about this, we were given an offer for SIMOSE. The site was just the right size for the villas, so we proposed to redesign them and it was accepted.

Hara   Four of the Forest Villas are reproductions of existing Case Study Houses, while the other Forest Villas and five of the Waterfront Villas were newly designed for the site. Every room has a completely different quality.

Ban   I think the difference between the experimental residential buildings I designed in my early days and the new buildings I built later as I matured while visiting and staying at various accommodations is quite apparent, reflecting the thirty-year difference in my experience. Also, the reason we designed all the buildings differently is because we wanted people to stay at a different building each night during the few days of their stay or enjoy

原 「森のヴィラ」の4棟は既存のケース・スタディ・ハウスの再現、他1棟と「水辺のヴィラ」の5棟はこの地のために新しく設計された建築ですが、どの部屋も全く違う良さがありますよね。

坂 初期に設計した実験的な住宅建築と、その後いろいろな施設を泊まり歩いて成熟してきた頃につくった新しい建築と、僕の中でも約30年の経験の差があるので、けっこう違いが現れていると思います。またデザインをすべて変えたのは、連泊や再訪の楽しみづくりでもあるんです。たとえば旅館に行くと大体どの部屋もお風呂が似ていると感じていたので、今回は各部屋のお風呂をすべて違うデザインにしました。水辺のヴィラも、外観こそ同じですが内装がすべて異なります。地元の工務店と1棟ずつつくっていったので、施工は本当に大変だったのですが。

原 一方で、すべての部屋に心地のいい開放感がありますよね。外気と居住空間を完璧にシャットアウトするのではなく、開放していくという考え方でしょうか。春とか秋とかシーズンによっては内と外の空間を融通させたくなるときがあります。西洋式のホテルでもなく、日本式の旅館でもなく、自然とどう対峙するかということに対して日本固有の空間づくりが突き詰められているように感じました。

坂 気持ちのいい場所って世界のどこの国の人にとっても共通で、縁側のような外と内の中間的な領域ですよね。だから僕はいかに家の内と外を連続させ、気持ちのいい空間をつくるかということを常々考えています。海は一日の中でも表情ががらりと変わりますからね。天気によっても、季節によっても全然違いますし。訪れるたびに、新しい発見をしてもらえたらいいなと思います。

revisiting the site in the future. For example, whenever I visit ryokans (Japanese-style inns,) I feel that all the rooms have similar baths. So, I designed all the baths in each room to be different. Also, the Waterfront Villas are identical on the outside, but the interiors are all different. We built them one by one with a local contractor, so the construction was quite challenging.

Hara   Meanwhile, all the rooms have a pleasant open atmosphere. I guess the idea is to not completely shut out the living space from the outside air, but to open it up. Depending on the seasons, like spring or autumn, we may want to integrate the inside and outside spaces. I feel that the buildings are neither a Western-style hotel nor a Japanese-style ryokan, but instead reflect a uniquely Japanese approach to space creation in relation to how we interact with nature.

Ban   People from all parts of the world seem to share the same sense of a pleasant place, an intermediate area between the outside and inside, like an engawa (a type of veranda that wraps around the outer edge of a traditional Japanese house.) That's why I always think about how to make the inside and outside of a house continuous and create a pleasant space. The ocean changes its appearance dramatically over the course of a day, depending on the weather, and the seasons. I hope visitors will discover something new every time they visit.

静かな内海という、強烈な資源

原　瀬戸内海はいいですよね、波が静かで。それって実はものすごく大きな価値です。瀬戸内国際芸術祭などに海外の人たちが訪れると船上の情景にひときわ感動するそうです。多島海というとエーゲ海などが連想されますが、あちらは島と島との間隔が離れていて、雄大ではあるものの瀬戸内海のように細やかに散在している群島を眺めることはできない。こういった静かな海があるってことは、日本にとって強烈な財産なんですね。そう考えると、300とも600とも言われる無人島も、意外と大きな可能性に見えてくるのではないでしょうか。

坂　宿泊施設という観点でも、やっぱり泊まるだけではなくプラスアルファで楽しめることが、その場所その町であるといいですよね。そういった意味でSIMOSEは瀬戸内地域の新しい拠点になったと思うので、これから船の移動が活発になるとか、より他の町との連携が活発になるとか、点と点がつながっていくようなことが起こってほしいと思います。

原　昔は瀬戸内海も横の動きと言いますか、本州と四国の連絡だけじゃなくて島と島の間の移動がすごく盛んだったわけですが、いまは干上がってきてしまいましたよね。日本人って船酔いする民族なのかなと思ってしまうくらい、船の愉楽がないんですよ。水辺に囲まれているけれど、意外とハーバーのような場所がない。かといって海外のクルーザー文化を日本に入れてくればよいというわけではなくて、たとえば宮島からSIMOSEに船で来ちゃおう、みたいな想像も自然と湧いてくるのですが、そういった移動の仕方をもう一度蘇らせると瀬戸内という地域の可能性が広がってくるのではないでしょうか。

坂　本州側でも、車で海岸沿いを走っているといちばん景色のいいところに廃工場がたくさんあって。よく見るとけっこう鉄骨が美しいものもあるのでリノベーションできるといいのですが、土地の用途に制限があって難しいのが現状です。そういった資源が活かせるようになるとまた一皮剥けるんじゃないかと思うんですけどね。

A Calm Inland Sea, a Powerful Resource

Hara   The Seto Inland Sea is nice, with its gentle waves, and it is actually a valuable asset. When people from overseas visit the Setouchi International Art Festival and other events, they are particularly impressed by the scenery from the boat. The archipelagic sea is associated with places like the Aegean Sea, but the distance between islands there is much greater. It is magnificent but does not offer the unique vista of closely scattered archipelagos like the Seto Inland Sea. The very presence of such a calm sea is a powerful asset for Japan. In this light, we may find an unexpected great potential in the three-hundred to six-hundred uninhabited islands there.

Ban   I think accommodation facilities should offer something extra to enjoy in each place and town, rather than simply offering places to stay. In this sense, now that SIMOSE has become a new hub for the Setouchi region, I hope to see an increase in boat traffic and more active cooperation with other towns to connect the dots.

Hara   In the past, the Seto Inland Sea was very active in terms of transverse mobility, or transportation between islands as well as between Honshu and Shikoku, but it has dried up since. The Japanese people don't seem to cherish the joy of boating to the extent that I wonder if they easily get seasick. Japan is surrounded by water, but there are surprisingly few waterfront destinations such as harbors. But that does not mean we should simply bring the overseas cruising culture to Japan. For example, we could naturally imagine coming to SIMOSE from Miyajima by boat. If we revive such a way of traveling, I think it would expand the possibilities of the Setouchi region.

Ban   Also, on the Honshu (main island) side, we come across many abandoned factories in the most scenic areas when driving along the coast. Looking closely, some of them have quite beautiful steel frames. It would be great to renovate them, but it is difficult due to the restrictions on land use. I think leveraging such resources will lead to breakthroughs.

Hara   I agree. The world is experiencing an "epoch of playful traveling" now, and people are beginning to travel around to explore the attractions unique to each region. I don't like words like inbound travelers, the affluent, or luxury, but it will be important to gain the interest and respect of people who have the intelligence and the eyes to understand the qualities of different cultures and are willing to pay a reasonable price for them, so people can find pride in the land they live in.

Ban   After all, it is foreigners who discover them. When one lives in Japan, one may take for granted the good qualities of the climate, culture, and landscape, and not be inclined to make the most of them. I think we can enrich them more if we can quickly discover the things inherently rooted in that region and develop the land in a way that is not too large in scale.

原　そうですね。いま、世界は「遊動の時代」を迎えていて、その土地ならではの素晴らしさを味わうために人々が動き始めています。インバウンドや富裕層、ラグジュアリーといった言葉が僕はあまり好きではないのですが、異文化の良さを理解する目と知性を持ち、それに対して相応の対価を払える人々から興味と敬意をいただくこと、またそれによって自分たちが住まう土地に誇りを見出していくことが大切になってくるはずです。

坂　結局、発見するのは外国人ですよね。日本に住んでいると風土も文化も良さがどこか当たり前になっていて、それを活用しようという気にならないのかもしれません。その土地にもともと根付いているものをいち早く見つけて、規模が大きくなりすぎないように開発していくともっと豊かになっていくように思います。

原　日本はGDP第四位の工業国と思われがちですが、実際は国土の大半が自然なんですよね。四方を海に囲まれた島国でありながら、山も国土の約65％と、フィンランドに次いで世界第二位の森林率を誇っている。そこに千数百年にわたる文化の蓄積があるわけですから、そういったことをどうやって未来の資源にしていくかということを考えると、やるべきことはたくさんあると思います。観光というのは、人が動いていくところをどうやって受け止めるかということなので、そのひとつの拠点としてSIMOSEも発見してもらえたらいいですね。

Hara   While Japan is often regarded as an industrialized country with the fourth largest GDP, the majority of the country's land is covered with nature. While it is an island nation surrounded by the sea on all sides, it also boasts mountains occupying about 65% of its land, making it the second most forested country in the world after Finland. On top of that, since it has more than a thousand years of cultural accumulation, there is much work to be done in terms of how to make these into resources for the future. Tourism is about how to receive people moving from one place to another, so I hope they discover SIMOSE as one of the destination points.

データ

SIMOSE（下瀬美術館、Simose Art Garden Villa、SIMOSE French Restaurant）

所在地		広島県大竹市晴海2丁目10-50
建主		丸井産業

規模	敷地面積	46,412.74m²
	建築面積	6,228.92m²
	延床面積	7,421.90m²
	建蔽率	13.42%（許容60%）
	容積率	15.99%（許容200%）

敷地条件	地域地区	都市計画区域内（市街化区域）、商業地域、法22条地域、地区計画（晴海二丁目区域）
	道路幅員	北側13.0m
	駐車台数	83台（車椅子用2台）

設計・監理	建築・家具	坂茂建築設計
	構造	KAP、村田龍馬設計所（Villa 6-10）
	設備	森村設計
	ランドスケープ	アースケイプ
	照明	Lumimedia lab
	造成	日野原富士コンサルタント
	VI・サイン・Web	日本デザインセンター
	テキスタイル	NUNO
	監理	丸井産業一級建築士事務所

施工　　　鹿島建設 中国支店（下瀬美術館、SIMOSE French Restaurant）
　　　　　大和建設（Simose Art Garden Villa）

工程（設計／施工）
2019年9月〜2021年4月／2021年5月〜2023年1月（美術館）
2019年9月〜2022年2月／2022年3月〜2023年1月（レストラン棟）
2019年9月〜2022年2月／2022年3月〜2023年3月（Villa全棟、レセプション棟）

建築概要（構造／階数／延床面積）
下瀬美術館：地上2階 地下1階／計5,946.81m²（エントランス棟：鉄骨造＋木造／地上1階／808.83m²、企画展示棟：鉄筋コンクリート造 一部プレストレストコンクリート造／鉄骨造／地上2階、1,763.39m²、管理棟：鉄骨造／地上2階／2,231.80m²、可動展示棟：鉄骨造＋鋼製台船造／地上1階／784.08m²）
Villa 1　ダブル・ルーフの家：鉄骨造／地上2階／103.19 m²
Villa 2　壁のない家：RC造、一部鉄骨造／地上1階／113.99m²
Villa 3　十字壁の家：RC造、一部鉄骨造、一部木造／地上3階／83.37m²
Villa 4　家具の家：木造／地上1階／107.21m²
Villa 5　紙の家：紙管構造、一部鉄骨造／地上1階／100.00m²
Villa 6-10　キールステックの家A-E：木造／地上1階／54.22m²
レセプション棟：木造／地上2階／103.19m²
レストラン棟：鉄骨造、一部木造／地上1階　地下1階／616.43m²
カート置場：木造／地上1階／28.60m²
駐輪場：木造／地上1階／16.80m²

設備（環境配慮技術）
太陽光発電305kW（全量直消費）（美術館、レストラン棟）

Data

SIMOSE (Simose Art Museum, Simose Art Garden Villa, SIMOSE French Restaurant)

Location: 2-10-50 Harumi, Otake-shi, Hiroshima Prefecture
Owner: Marui Sangyo Co., Ltd.

Project Scale		
	Site area	46,412.74m^2
	Building area	6,228.92m^2
	Total floor area	7,421.90m^2
	Building coverage ratio	13.42% (maximum allowable ratio: 60%)
	Floor-area ratio	15.99% (maximum allowable ratio: 200%)

Site Conditions		
	Zoning district	Within the city planning area (urbanization area), commercial area, Article 22 area, district planning (Harumi 2-chome area)
	Road width	North side: 13.0m
	Number of parking spaces	83 (including 2 wheelchair-accessible spaces)

Design / Supervision	Architecture / furniture	Shigeru Ban Architects
	Structure	KAP, Ryoma Murata Building Studio (Villa 6-10)
	Building equipment	P. T. Morimura and Associates
	Landscape	Earthscape
	Lighting	Lumimedia Lab
	Landfill	Hinoharafuji Consultant Inc.
	VI / signage / website	Nippon Design Center, Inc.
	Textile	NUNO
	Supervision	Marui Sangyo First Class Architect

Construction   Kajima Corporation Chugoku Branch (Simose Art Museum, SIMOSE French Restaurant)
Daiwa Construction Co., Ltd. (Simose Art Garden Villa)

Construction Schedule (Design / Construction)
September 2019-April 2021 / May 2021-January 2023 (Museum)
September 2019-February 2022 / March 2022-January 2023 (Restaurant Building)
September 2019-February 2022 / March 2022-March 2023 (Villas, Reception Building)

Buildings Summary (Structure / Number of Stories / Total Floor Area)
Simose Art Museum: 2 stories above ground, 1 story underground / 5,946.81 m^2 in total (Entrance Hall: steel and wooden construction / 1 story above ground / 808.83m^2, Special Exhibition Building: reinforced concrete construction, partly prestressed concrete construction / steel construction / 2 stories above ground, 1,763.39m^2, Administration Building: steel construction / 2 stories above ground / 2,231.80m^2, Movable Exhibition Buildings: steel construction + steel barge construction / 1 story above ground / 784.08m^2)
Villa 1   House of Double-Roof: steel construction / 2 stories above ground / 103.19 m^2
Villa 2   Wall-Less House: reinforced concrete construction, partially steel construction / 1 story above ground / 113.99 m^2
Villa 3   Cross Wall House: reinforced concrete construction, partially steel construction / 3 stories above ground / 83.37 m^2
Villa 4   Furniture House: wooden construction / 1 story above ground / 107.21 m^2
Villa 5   Paper House: Paper tube construction, partially steel construction / 1 story above ground / 100.00 m^2
Villa 6-10   Kielsteg House A-E: wooden construction / 1 story above ground / 54.22 m^2
Reception Building: wooden construction / 2 stories above ground / 103.19 m^2
Restaurant Building: steel construction, partially wooden construction / 1 story above ground, 1 story underground / 616.43 m^2
Cart parking: wooden construction / 1 story above ground / 28.60 m^2
Bicycle parking: wooden construction / 1 story above ground / 16.80 m^2

Equipment (environmental technology)
solar power generation 305kW (Total direct consumption) (Museum and Restaurant Building)

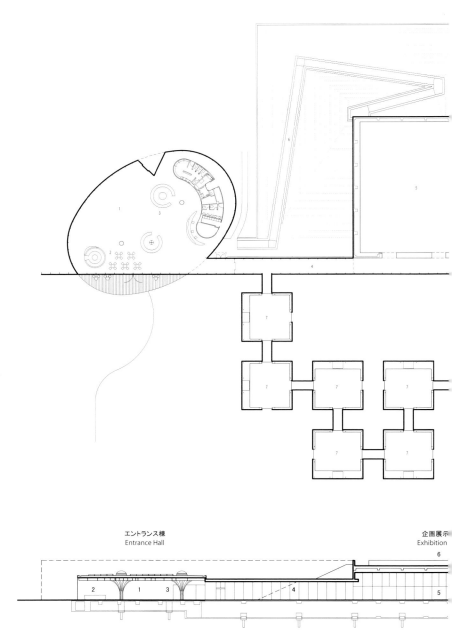

エントランス棟
Entrance Hall

企画展示
Exhibition

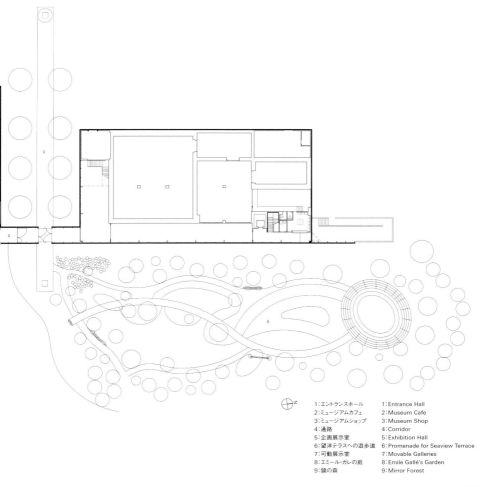

1:エントランスホール	1:Entrance Hall
2:ミュージアムカフェ	2:Museum Cafe
3:ミュージアムショップ	3:Museum Shop
4:通路	4:Corridor
5:企画展示室	5:Exhibition Hall
6:望洋テラスへの遊歩道	6:Promenade for Seaview Terrace
7:可動展示室	7:Movable Galleries
8:エミール・ガレの庭	8:Emile Gallé's Garden
9:鏡の森	9:Mirror Forest

Scale=1/700

管理棟
Administration Building

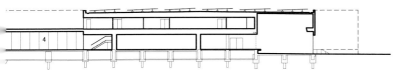

1:エントランスホール	1:Entrance Hall
2:ミュージアムカフェ	2:Museum Cafe
3:ミュージアムショップ	3:Museum Shop
4:通路	4:Corridor
5:企画展示室	5:Exhibition Hall
6:望洋テラス	6:Seaview Terrace

Scale=1/700

Data

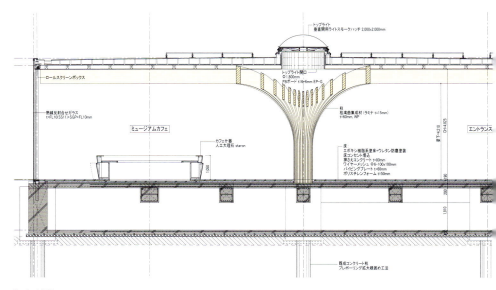

Scale=1/150

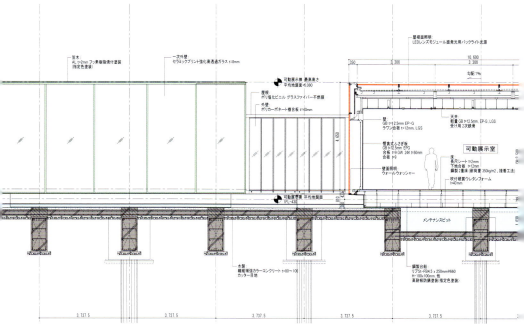

Scale=1/150

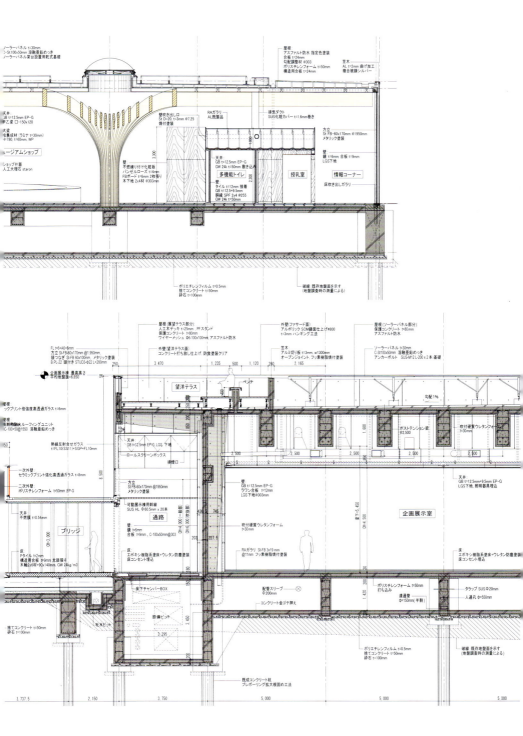

クレジット

財団概要	財団名	一般財団法人下瀬美術館

代表理事　下瀬ゆみ子
設立年月日　2018年9月6日
事業内容　美術工芸品の保存、公開、調査研究、及び展覧会等の文化活動を行う
所在地　（財団）　〒733-8616 広島県広島市西区商工センター1-1-46
　　　　（美術館）　〒739-0622 広島県大竹市晴海2-10-50
お問い合わせ　Tel: 0827-94-4000
関連会社　丸井産業株式会社

建築設計

坂 茂（ばん・しげる）
1957年東京生まれ。アメリカで建築を学び、東京、パリ、ニューヨークに事務所を構える。紙管や木材を使った革新的な建築で知られている。1995年にNGO「Voluntary Architects' Network (VAN)」を設立し、世界各地での災害支援に数多く貢献している。プリツカー建築賞（2014年）、マザー・テレサ社会正義賞（2017年）、アストゥリアス皇太子賞平和部門（2022年）を受賞。代表作はポンピドゥー・センター・メス（2010年）、紙の大聖堂（2013年）、富士山世界遺産センター（2017年）、禅坊 靖寧（2022年）。慶應義塾大学環境情報学部教授（2001-2008年、2015-2023年）、京都芸術大学大学院教授（芸術研究科）、2023年4月より芝浦工業大学特別招聘教授。

アートディレクション

原 研哉（はら・けんや）
1958年生まれ。グラフィックデザイナー。日本デザインセンター代表。武蔵野美術大学教授。主な仕事に、「RE-DESIGN：日常の21世紀」展、「HAPTIC」「SENSE WARE」「Ex-formation」など展覧会や教育活動。長野オリンピックの開・閉会式プログラムや、愛知万博のプロモーションのデザイン。2002年より無印良品のアートディレクション。外務省「JAPAN HOUSE」総合プロデューサーなど多数。著書に『DESIGNING DESIGN』(Lars Müller Publishers)、『白』（中央公論新社）、『日本のデザイン』（岩波新書）、『低空飛行 この国のかたちへ』（岩波書店）など。

ランドスケープ

団塚栄喜（だんづか・えいき）
1963年大分県佐伯市大入島生まれ。風景司。モノ派を代表する関根伸夫氏に師事、1999年にアースケイプを設立し、人と自然との関係性を創りだす仕掛けをデザインと捉え、体験の媒体となるデザインワークを行う。「MIYASHITA PARK」、台湾雲林県斗六総合運動公園など国内外の大型施設のランドスケープやアートワークを手掛ける。都市景観大賞、SDA賞など受賞多数。

レストラン監修

小沢貴彦（おざわ・たかひこ）
1947年横浜生まれ。「キャラバンサライ」「ホテルオークラ」を経て「ラ・マレ」「ア・ラ・タブール」「ア・タント」の料理長を務めたのち、東京都港区白金台にフレンチレストラン「OZAWA」を開店。フランス料理界の重鎮として、素材の扱い方や盛り付けなどに独特の世界を作り出す。

テキスタイル

須藤玲子（すどう・れいこ）
茨城県石岡市生まれ。株式会社布代表。東京造形大学名誉教授。毎日デザイン賞、ロスコー賞、円空大賞等受賞。日本の伝統的な染織技術から現代の先端技術までを駆使し、新しいテキスタイルづくりを行う。作品はニューヨーク近代美術館、メトロポリタン美術館、ヴィクトリア&アルバート博物館他に永久保存されている。

Credits

Foundation Overview	Foundation Name:	General Incorporated Association Simose Art Museum
	Representative Director:	Yumiko Shimose
	Establishment date:	September 6, 2018
	Description of operations:	Preserving and exhibiting arts and crafts, conducting research and studies, and holding exhibitions and other cultural activities.
	Location:	(Foundation) 1-1-46 Shoko Center, Nishi-ku, Hiroshima-shi, Hiroshima 733-8616
		(Museum) 2-10-50 Harumi, Otake-shi, Hiroshima 739-0622
	Inquiry:	Tel: +81-827-94-4000
	Affiliated Company:	Marui Sangyo Co., Ltd.

Architectural Design

Shigeru BAN   Known for his architecture using paper tubes and innovative wooden structures. Established the NGO Voluntary Architects' Network (VAN) in 1995, and received the Pritzker Architecture Prize (2014), the Mother Teresa Social Justice Award (2017), and the Princess of Asturias Award for Concord (2022) for his numerous contributions to disaster relief around the world. His representative works include Center Pompidou-Metz, Metz, France (2010), Cardboard Cathedral, Christchurch, New Zealand (2013), Oita Prefectural Art Museum, Oita, Japan (2015), Mt. Fuji World Heritage Centre, Shizuoka, Japan (2017), and ZEN Wellness SEINEI, Awaji Island, Hyogo, Japan (2022). Serves as Professor at the Faculty of Environment and Information Studies, Keio University (2001-2008), Professor at Graduate School, Kyoto University of the Arts (Art Studies), and Special Guest Professor at Shibaura Institute of Technology since April 2023.

Art Direction

Kenya HARA   Born in 1958. Graphic Designer. He serves as President of Nippon Design Center. Professor at Musashino Art University. His major works include exhibitions and educational activities, including the "RE-DESIGN: Everyday Life in the 21st Century" exhibition, "HAPTIC," "SENSE WARE," and "Ex-formation," Nagano Olympics opening and closing ceremony programs, Aichi Expo promotion design among others. He has been engaged in the art direction of MUJI since 2002. Chief Creative Director of the Japan House project by the Ministry of Foreign Affairs. His publications include *DESIGNING DESIGN* (Lars Müller Publishers), *Shiro* (Chuokoron Shinsha), *Nippon no Design* (Iwanami Shinsho), and *Teiku-hiko: Kono Kuni no Katachi e* (Iwanami Shoten.)

Landscape

Eiki DANZUKA   Born in 1963 in Onyujima, Saiki-shi, Oita Prefecture. Earthscape Designer. Studied under Nobuo Sekine, one of the representative figures of the Mono-ha, and founded Earthscape in 1999. He sees design as a mechanism for creating a relationship between people and nature and undertakes design work as a medium for experience. He has created landscapes and artwork for large-scale facilities in Japan and abroad, including MIYASHITA PARK and Douliu Sports Park in Yunlin County, Taiwan. He has received numerous awards, including the Urban Landscape Award and the SDA Award.

Restaurant Supervision

Takahiko OZAWA   Born in Yokohama, Kanagawa Prefecture in 1947. Worked at "Caravanserai" and "Hotel Okura" before serving as head chef at "La Marais," "A La Table," and "A Tanto," and opened the French restaurant "OZAWA" in Shirokanedai, Minato-ku, Tokyo. As a leading figure in the French culinary scene, he has created a distinctive world of his own with through his unique handling of ingredients and culinary presentation.

Textiles

Reiko SUDO   Born in Ishioka, Ibaraki Prefecture. Design Director, NUNO Corporation. Professor Emeritus at Tokyo Zokei University. Recipient of numerous awards including the Mainichi Design Award, Roscoe Award and Enku Prize. She creates new textiles using traditional Japanese dyeing and weaving techniques and cutting-edge modern technology. Her works are in the permanent collections at the Museum of Modern Art in New York, Metropolitan Museum of Art, Victoria & Albert Museum, and many other institutions worldwide.

アートに触れる場、SIMOSE

丸井産業株式会社　代表取締役

下瀬ゆみ子

1958年に父と母と共に創業した広島の地で、SIMOSEのプロジェクトは2016年にスタートし、丸井産業創業60周年を機に本格的に始動いたしました。私たちは下瀬コレクションの展示を通して、公共の福祉に貢献したいと考えております。地元広島の地域の皆さま、そして日本各地、海外からのお客さまにお越しいただき、美術品に触れ親しんでいただく場としてふさわしいアート複合施設にするため、ともに世界的な評価を受ける坂 茂氏に設計を、原研哉氏に施設のコミュニケーションデザインをお願いいたしました。それから約8年の歳月をかけて2023年春、ついに完成へと至りました。

宮島と瀬戸内海を望むこの素晴らしい土地を、訪れていただいた方はまた再び、そして本書をご覧になった方へも是非お越しいただけますと嬉しいです。

最後に、父母から受けてきた恩顧に感謝するとともに、建設および開館に際し、ご尽力を賜りました関係各位のご高配に敬意と感謝を申し上げます。

SIMOSE: A P ace to Experience Art

Marui Sangyo Corporation President

Yumiko SHIMOSE

The SIMOSE project began in 2016 in Hiroshima, where my father, mother, and I started Marui Sangyo together in 1958, and got into full swing on the occasion of Marui Sangyo's 60th anniversary. We hope to contribute to the public welfare through the exhibition of the SIMOSE Collection. To create an art complex suitable for residents of Hiroshima as well as visitors from all over Japan and abroad to experience and familiarize themselves with works of art, we commissioned internationally acclaimed architect Shigeru Ban for the architectural design and also an internationally acclaimed designer Kenya Hara for the communication design of the facility. After about eight years of work, the project was finally completed in the spring of 2023.

We hope that those who have visited this spectacular site overlooking Miyajima and Seto Inland Sea will return, and that those who have read this book will also visit us.

In closing, I would like to express my gratitude for the patronage I have received from my parents as well as my respect and gratitude to all those involved for their efforts in the construction and opening of the museum.

SIMOSEに訪れる人々を出迎える自立式サイン。ゆるやかに湾曲した3枚のプレートは、瀬戸内海を吹き抜ける風を受けて穏やかに回ります。この場所に流れる時間を象徴するようです。
A freestanding sign welcomes visitors to SIMOSE. The three gently curved plates rotate serenely with the breeze crossing the Seto Inland Sea. They seem to symbolize the time that flows through this place.

SIMOSE: A Place to Experience Art

五感がそよぐ日。

海へ抜けるアートの庭、SIMOSE。
美術、工芸、建築、食、自然、
その知らなかった体験をするたびに
五感がゆらぎ、思考がめぐり、
想像がふくらんでいくようです。
自分の内に風をとおすような、
気持ちのいい日をお過ごしください。

A day to stir the senses.

SIMOSE is a garden of art by the sea.
Art, craftsmanship, architecture, cuisine, nature
fresh experiences arouse the senses,
stimulate the mind, and expand the imagination.
Enjoy the pleasure of a day
like a breeze that courses through you.

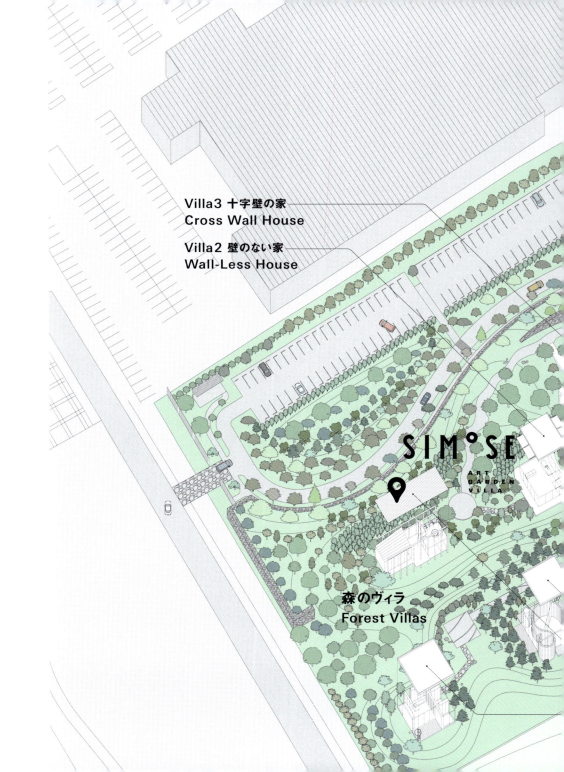

Villa3 十字壁の家
Cross Wall House

Villa2 壁のない家
Wall-Less House

SIMOSE
ART GARDEN VILLA

森のヴィラ
Forest Villas

写真クレジット | Photographic Credits (t=top, b=bottom, l=left, r=right)

関口尚志 | Takashi SEKIGUCHI: pp.002-003, 010-016, 021b, 023t, 026-027, 030-031, 034-035, 038-039t, 040l, 042-043l, 045lt, 045b, 046b, 050-051, 058b, 062-063, 067-070, 074-075, 079b, 083b, 087, 095, 098-100t, 102-103, 112-116l, 120-121, 124, 137-139, 144

平井広行 | Hiroyuki HIRAI: pp.004-009, 018-019, 021t, 023b, 024, 036-037, 038b, 040r-041, 043r, 060, 071-073, 076-079t, 080-083t, 084-086, 088-089, 091-094, 096-097, 100b-101, 110-111, 116r-117, 122, 126

下瀬美術館 | Simose Art Museum: pp.028-029, 032-033, 045rt

中戸川史明 | Shimei NAKATOGAWA: pp.044, 046t, 048-049, 106-109, 118-119

村上宗一郎 | Soichiro MURAKAMI: p.053

日本デザインセンター | Nippon Design Center, Inc.: pp.054-055, 066, 079b, 104

丸井産業 | Marui Sangyo Co,. Ltd.: p.056

SIMOSE　建築とデザイン

2024年10月15日　第1刷発行

編著者　　SIMOSE編集委員会
　　　　　坂茂建築設計：坂 茂、菅井啓太、山内晃洋、中村有利
　　　　　日本デザインセンター：原 研哉、中村晋平、浅井花怜、矢崎 花
　　　　　鹿島出版会：相川幸二、久保田昭子
協力　　　下瀬美術館、Shimose A&R
発行者　　新妻 充
発行所　　鹿島出版会
　　　　　〒104-0061
　　　　　東京都中央区銀座6-17-1銀座六丁目-SQUARE 7階
　　　　　03-6264-2301　振替00160-2-180883
印刷・製本　サンエムカラー
ブックデザイン　原 研哉＋中村晋平＋浅井花怜＋矢崎 花
英文翻訳　　坂本和子、サム・ホールデン（pp.1, 140）
英文校正　　織部晴崇

©SIMOSE Compilation Committee 2024, Printed in Japan
ISBN978-4-306-04717-4 C3052

落丁・乱丁本はお取り替えいたします。
本書の無断複製（コピー）は著作権法上での例外を除き禁じられています。また、代行業者等に依頼してスキャンやデジタル化することは、たとえ個人や家庭内の利用を目的とする場合でも著作権法違反です。

本書の内容に関するご意見・ご感想は下記までお寄せ下さい。
http://www.kajima-publishing.co.jp/
info@kajima-publishing.co.jp

管理棟
Administration Building

企画展示棟
Exhibition Hall

望洋テラス
Seaview Terrace

エミール・ガレの庭
Emile Gallé's Garden

SIM°SE
ART
GARDEN
VILLA

ション
ption

エントランス棟
Entrance Hall

下瀬美術館
SIMOSE
ART MUSEUM

可動展示室
Movable Galleries

A   B   C   D   E

水辺のヴィラ
Waterfront Villas

Villa6-10 キールステックの家
Kielsteg House

SIM°SE

French Restaurant

Discover local ingredients and
the essence of food.

ハーブ・ガーデン
Herb Garden

Villa5 紙の家
Paper House

Villa1 ダブル・ルーフの家
House of Double-Roof

Villa4 家具の家
Furniture House

SIM°SE